Real Mentors Tell You This

Real Mentors Tell You This

Regina Darmoni

To order additional copies of this book, contact:
Xlibris Corporation
1-888-795-4274
www.Xlibris.com
Orders@Xlibris.com
39067

CONTENTS

Part I: Lessons Learned

Chapter 1:   Real Mentors Tell You: The Real Secret to Success—Execute!....15

Chapter 2:   Real Mentors Tell You: Inspect, Don't Expect 27

Chapter 3:   Real Mentors Tell You: If You Can't Net it, You Don't Know it 39

Chapter 4:   Real Mentors Tell You: Anticipate the Obvious 59
  • Your vision
  • Everyone else's vision

Chapter 5:   Real Mentors Tell You: The Verb's the Thing.....................67
  • Leadership Language
  • Languish Language

Chapter 6:   Real Mentors Tell You: There's an Art to Arguing 77
  • Grace Under Fire & While Firing
  • When to Talk
  • When to Shut Up

Chapter 7:   Real Mentors Tell You: Collaborate to Win 89
  • When Colleagues Will Help You, When They Won't
  • Attitude for Altitude
  • How to REALLY Build a Network

Chapter 8:   Real Mentors Tell You: Enlarge and Charge.....................107
  • SWOT: Yourself and Your Competition
  • Right Move, Wrong Time
  • Your First Management Job
  • Distinguishing Experiences

Part II: Questions Asked

Chapter 9: Mentoring Mojo 121
- When You're in Trouble
- Needing Feedback vs Being Needy
- Other Selected Topics

Chapter 10: Pulse and Surge: How to make your vision of you happen..... 147

Sample Documents 153
- Your Annual Business Commitment Plan
- Your Annual Business Commitment Plan Results
- Your Career Development Plan
- Email: A "do" and a "don't"

Afterword The Best Of...161

DEDICATION

I am able to write this book on mentoring because I have been so generously mentored myself—by senior managers, by peers, by colleagues who modeled successful behaviors, and by good friends offering caring, solid advice. I am immensely grateful to the following folks who have given me pivotal career opportunities, who kept advising me long after I'd left their 'class,' and who continue to model leadership behavior every day: Dr. John Acocella, Dr. Thomas Caulfield, Michael J. Cadigan, Dr. Henry Geipel, John Waite, Lisa Beilstein, Tom Reeves, Geoffrey Akiki, Scottie Ginn, Fred Glasgow, and John Ditoro. I also want to acknowledge and thank my first corporate hero, Robert I. Feldman, who showed all the new hires of 1980-1982 just how much could be accomplished in a previously-unheard-of three years. We all began to dream big dreams because of Rob.

To the Fellas

My son, David, as can be expected of a first-born, can already do almost everything I recommend in this book. If only I could only get him to clean his room! I shall never forget his sincere support in early 2005 when he said, "Don't optimize around me, I am almost out of here." He has an enormous capacity for generosity and, I think plans to take over the world.

As for Julien, my number two "free-spirited", musical boy, not only do I not know if he would follow any of the advice in this book, I am not alone in wondering if he will even read it! Despite his lack of interest and enthusiasm for my work—and his protests to the contrary—he will probably wind up being an engineer. Given that, I strongly recommend that he read this book and yes, go ahead, set it to music.

Peter, you came late to this party, but your arrival *made* it a party! Thank you for all the support, encouragement and fort breaks! Now that this book is finally done, I can go on dates again. This time, I am thankful that someone was willing to "wait"!

Edited by Janet Hubbard-Brown

FOREWORD

I wrote this book for new professional hires, but anyone in the corporate world who is not yet having the success they desire or envisioned for themselves can potentially benefit from reading it.

My editor, Janet Hubbard-Brown, tells me that I have invented a new word, "mentee." Janet, in her experienced and professional largesse, has advised me that while "mentee" does work, "protégé" might be a reasonable substitute and furthermore, already exists as a word! With that, it is my pleasure to introduce the word "mentee" and declare, after decades of working with incredibly innovative engineers, "Finally, I'm an inventor!"

INTRODUCTION

You have a mentor, but what exactly is it that the two of you are accomplishing together? What do you actually discuss? Do you meet dutifully each month or each quarter to discuss your thoughts on your career progression or lack thereof? Do you explore reasonable "next positions" for you? Do you evaluate the pros and cons of your going back to school for that MBA or perhaps an M.S.? Is an overseas assignment a good idea? Should you take job A over job B? How can you become a manager, top scientist, CFO, or executive?

These are all perfectly legitimate topics; after all, a mentor has achieved some level of success and should be perfectly capable of answering such routine questions. However, I submit that if this is all that is happening between you and your mentor, then you are not taking advantage of the wealth of experience mentors can provide. These "going to the next level" discussions are fine when the basics are covered, but I suspect that most people are not getting the basics covered. I question the usefulness and breadth of the feedback we employees get, especially the limited feedback that we have come to accept when "going to the next level" discussions occur with our mentors. I also suspect that many employees are not hearing about routine "blocking and tackling" improvement techniques that can help them to become more successful and more appreciated in their current positions, as well as help them increase their opportunities to be considered for (and win!) growth positions.

I think it reasonable to expect to be told what types of experiences we need to have in order to climb the career ladder, and where those experiences can most likely be had. Typically, we are given reasonable timeframes in which we can expect a promotion to occur, contacts to consult for more information, and/or background on a topic that may interest us. Our mentors may make a few phone calls on our behalf. But is that it? Is that all there is? Depending on where you are in your career, that may be sufficient. But if you are a new employee, or an employee who is **not** having the success you had hoped for, you may need more active mentoring.

I believe that mentoring is a "hands-on" assignment and that a good mentor will actively seek out his mentees and observe their performance in their own element. This observation forms the basis of an on-going meaningful and results-driven conversation. In addition to passing on the attributes that have contributed to his or her own success, the mentor can customize "straight talk" based on observations of the mentee at work.

I envision a mentor who will tell you what you are you doing well and then make suggestions as to how you can perform even better. Good mentors point out what isn't working, and then teach you how to correct those problem areas. A good mentor should be a terrific complement to your manager and must be capable of having frank and direct conversations with you. These conversations should be an on-going exchange that stresses winning in the workplace, planning, execution, inspection, articulation, the need to net, presenting data, presenting oneself, self-examination and corrective action, ownership, leadership, and a "can-do" attitude. Engaged mentors tell you how to anticipate and prepare for "obvious" questions, when to speak up and when to shut up, how to collaborate to win, about personal resiliency, gut checks, ego checks, and derailment factors.

If you are not having these kinds of talks with your mentors, you are not being actively mentored and if you are not being actively mentored, you should know, **real mentors tell you this** . . .

PART I

Lessons Learned

CHAPTER 1

Real Mentors Tell You:
The Real Secret to Success—Execute!

What does it take?

Senior managers are often asked to share their one, fail-safe, sure-fire secret to success. The questioner is typically seeking a blazingly insightful response that has heretofore been hidden from his/her unseeing eyes. The answer is actually quite straightforward: sign up to deliver meaningful or critical contributions to your business, and execute well to deliver them.

Executing well means meeting your commitments in a legal and ethical manner, delivering your work either on budget and schedule, or surpassing both—while at the same time avoiding client dissatisfaction and a trail littered with abused colleagues. Executing well means building trust; the trust of your management team, colleagues, and clients. Trust leads to increased responsibility; delivering on the increased responsibility engenders more trust and more responsibility; and the person enjoying this swirl of success derived from delivery, trust, and increased responsibility will eventually find herself on the receiving end of the business neophyte's eternal career question: what is the one real secret to success? While timing, networking and luck are often part of the equation in any success story, aside from whatever else may happen in your career—including whom you happen to know—the most satisfying way to achieve success and longevity in the business world is to execute well.

Executing

So called cliques and 'old boys networks', which now include women, exist at the office, and they can be an important source of information and affliative 'recognition'. However, I am convinced that even if you massively network, play a mean game of golf on the company team, and are the greatest contributor to team morale and a fantastic work climate, you won't be successful if you cannot be counted on to create, own, and deliver meaningful business commitments. Being the boss' confidante, babysitting his kids, standing up at her wedding, or donating a kidney to his beloved mother won't help you in the long run if you are not contributing to the business.

You can be lucky, you can be in the right place at the right time, you can have stellar credentials—all important, contributory factors—however, they are not going to buy you much if the status on your projects continuously read 'late' or 'under-performing'.

The one sure way to be successful and appreciated at your place of business is to make clear, precise commitments that align with the needs of your company's (or your division's) business, and to deliver them—at a minimum—on time and on budget. For example, it will not matter as much as you might think if you are the chief contributor to client satisfaction (admittedly critical) when your boss is measuring your performance on consistent double-digit revenue growth. Likewise, it will matter less than you think if you deliver double-digit revenue growth this year, yet that accomplishment is marred by unhappy clients— this occurring when the boss was looking for twenty percent improvement in client satisfaction! If your business is looking for a combination of growth and client satisfaction, for example, you need to commit to both, and deliver on both in order to be successful.

> *"Finish. Anyone can start, but not everyone can finish."*
> *—Dr John Acocella*

When he was coaching our over-worked, long-in-need-of-a-break team to deliver on some of our product development commitments, my former boss, John Acocella, rallied us with that call to arms. We were always exhorted to finish.

It's not hard to find impediments to finishing an assignment. Some people find that they become bored midway through a lengthy project. They may tire of on-going battles to retain funding, or they may perceive a lack of project importance, or become lethargic due to a simple lack of managerial attention. Sometimes, just the day in /day out grind of problems surfacing can drain an employee or team, with energy flagging due to yet another problematic qualification cycle, product development pass, or prolonged client negotiation. Senior management attention is diverted to the crisis of the day, or to a sexier project, and out of the glow of attention, commitments start to slip. Critical team members may request transfer to, or may be needed on some other project and, low on bandwidth, the team's commitment status suddenly turns into 'late.' It is at this point when you and your team, if you have one, must hold fast to the commitments you have made: you must deliver. Institutional memory is very long. Make sure your name is included in the "will deliver" portion of cache.

Fortunately, the path to successful delivery is consistent across organizations. It requires that you have a plan, know how to achieve the plan, and have committed owners and 'milestones' for everything that must be delivered according to the plan. It also means that if you need help, you acknowledge that in a timely manner, know where that help can be found, get it, and that you finish.

Making it happen

1. **Have a plan.** A committed, detailed plan is essential for anything you seriously aim to accomplish. Your plan must clearly state what it is you agree to accomplish (deliver $10M of revenue or $1M of profit, or deliver Product Awesome from the research lab to the manufacturing floor, etc) and include a realistic deadline and all resources that will be required. The plan is the reference point to which you and everyone on your team will be measured for the duration of your project commitment. Make sure that everyone who must contribute something to the success of your project knows you are counting on them, and more to the point, make sure that they are committed to your project and schedule. They must know specifically what you need, when you need it, and at what budget and quality level.

> *"Major in the Major, Don't Major in the Minor"*
> *—Fred Glasgow*

During the execution phase, the best possible status, of course, is to be performing according to the plan ("on plan"), or "exceeding the plan." It is acceptable to veer slightly from the plan, as long as you can demonstrate how you are quickly going to get back on, with minimal disruption to business objectives. Unless you are extremely and consistently lucky, trying to operate without a solid, committed plan, or operating solely with a high-level plan, means that you are willing to allow events to happen randomly. This is a recipe for failure and is to be avoided.

2. **Know how to achieve the plan.** You have your plan in place, now you must know how to go about actually implementing it. If you are in sales for, example, you probably have been given a sales target that you are expected to achieve. Your plan cannot be that you will simply make sales calls and develop deals until you achieve your "numbers." Sales leaders will tell you that in order to *guarantee* that they achieve their quotas *now* and position themselves later for successful future quarters, they must identify a list of clients for whom they have a potential solution ("the pipeline"). From this pipeline they quickly determine who among those clients is capable of executing a sale (i.e., does the client have adequate resources?), and which clients have a project that can close on the salesman's timeline (i.e, can the client close a deal this quarter?) This is called "qualifying the pipeline."

If the answer is "yes" to both of the above questions, these clients are put at the top of the salesperson's execution list. A successful salesperson knows that even this is not sufficient, for every industry has a "close rate" associated with its pipeline. A salesperson must generate X% more general leads, and Y% of qualified leads, in order to close enough deals to meet his target. Knowing those ratios for his industry—in addition to having the necessary sales skills and solutions, of course—is essential to having a rewarding sales period.

To paraphrase advice from Fred Glasgow, when executing, you have to know what's important, where to get the "biggest bang for your buck" and immediately focus on that. In the example above, sales people filling their prospect list with trivial deals would be representative of working towards an objective, while majoring in the minor. While small deals add up, in order to be successful a sales person needs to find bigger deals—in many cases, *transformational* deals. To produce extraordinary performance, an exemplary employee works the "big ticket" items first, instinctively knowing to "major in the major, and minor in the minor." No matter what line of business you are in, to be successful you must quickly find and attack the "major" items, and as we will see later, inspect the details.

3. **Assign owners and define key milestones.** Make a master control chart of key task milestones and designate owners who will be responsible for timely and appropriate achievement of those milestones. If there is a lengthy project development cycle, this control chart must contain a minimum of monthly milestones. A shorter delivery cycle can have weekly milestones. Each milestone owner should develop a control chart for their tasks—limited to key actions and owners and dates for each. For ease of review, all project milestones can be portrayed with a simple traffic light color scheme of Green/Yellow/Red. This simple code focuses attention at a glance. Code "green" obviously means that the milestone will be completed on time and on budget. Code "yellow" means that the milestone is in danger of being missed, while code "red" means that the milestone will not occur on time, or has been missed. Anything coded "yellow" requires immediate action. In order to improve the status of the project, specific improvement actions must be identified, along with their respective owners and closure dates. These must be reviewed and managed more regularly than they otherwise might have been. To avoid seeing "red," your

> *If what you are doing is not working, continuing to do more of the same will not suddenly improve your results.*

personal management and extra attention must continue until any yellow milestone returns to "green" status.

If a milestone is flagged "red" (and given what we just said about "yellow" status, "red" status should only happen as a result of something dramatic that is beyond your control or that of the team), you should already be getting help from senior management and/or other project managers who have available resources.

4. **Measure yourself often.** If you measure yourself and your team only to the major endpoint, you are likely to fail, and furthermore are guaranteed to be engaging in a madcap race of stressful activity at the end of the project schedule. Set reasonable schedules: don't assign project completion dates at the end of a quarter or around major holidays. If, for example, it becomes necessary to get colleagues to work extra hours or days to deliver on your commitments, it will be difficult to capture their full attention when December 23 rolls around.

5. **"Ring the bell" immediately if you foresee delays** or major impediments to completing your work on time or on budget. Don't wait to notify others, and don't wait to get help! It's okay to ask for help! If what you are doing is not working, doing more of the same won't suddenly improve results. It's not okay to avoid asking for help and allowing the project to fail or fall behind schedule—and the team with it. Your task is to execute. Speak up, get help, and get back on track—*fast*. Yes, it will be noticed if you have achieved your aims without having had to resort to getting help. When this happens, everyone will appreciate it for a minute or two.

> *Don't wait to get help, and if help is offered, it's generally best to take it.*

23

But if you even *think* that you need help, get it. You will not be penalized for asking for help, rather, you will be rewarded for executing. On the other hand, if you don't ask for help and end up failing to execute well, you are not going to be congratulated because you didn't ask for help. Worse, you will not be trusted to do the right thing (which is to ask for help when you need it) the next time around.

Don't try to be a hero by refusing to ask for help if you need it. Time is extremely precious—don't let it slip by. Acknowledge that you need help, and seek it immediately. By the way, if you are offered help, it is generally best to take it. Unless you are absolutely, 100% sure you can recover alone, take the assist. If you ultimately do not readily recover your project status, it will likely be recalled that you were offered help and did not accept it. You can save yourself time by identifying particular subject matter experts at the beginning of a project and notifying them of your objectives. Consulting with them from time to time is an excellent way to have expert input as you proceed—and—if you encounter problems and need their help later, they will have been apprised of your project and status already, and will not waste time a lot of time getting on board.

If you get off schedule, set reasonable expectations for getting back on schedule or budget. If you get a project schedule reprieve, don't compromise your credibility by re-committing to getting back on track in two days if you really believe you need two weeks. Give a realistic and honest assessment of where you are versus the plan and what you need to get back on track. Keep flying the cautionary flag until you are completely back under control, and never hide your lack of recovery.

6. **Finish.** At the end of the day, before you can think about your next 'power' assignment, you have to have demonstrated that you've earned it. That means you created a plan, made sure everyone involved agreed to perform according to the needs of the plan, closely managed your deliverables, and made them all happen.

   As important as "on time" and "on budget" milestone deliveries is the quality of the work you will deliver. In the next chapter, we will explore how to improve the odds of getting what you need from others when you need it, and how, once you have it, it is something you can actually use.

   For now, though, execute well.

Mentoring Maxim

Real Mentors Tell You:
Get up to Get it Done.

In our fast-paced world, we are accustomed to multi-tasking. In our quest to get things done, we email, we use instant messages, we leave voicemails. In performing these actions, we convince ourselves that we are "handling" things. Many of us have forgotten how to *manage by walking around*. If you need to close a task or project and you haven't heard from the person you've emailed, called, voice-mailed a few times, and IM'd, don't give up and simply resort to waiting for a call back. On the other hand, don't attempt to follow up by leaving another of the above-mentioned remote messages. Remember what I said earlier about doing more of the same when it isn't working? Already called his assistant? Don't risk alienating her by continuing to call. Instead, *get up* from your chair and go to your colleague's office and get your business closed. He isn't on the same campus or in the same city? Instead, if after a reasonable time has passed and you still haven't gotten a response, try to reach other people in your colleague's department or call the guy in the adjoining office or cubicle and ask him to leave a note on your elusive party's chair. It should be clear that you are doing all that you can to reach him or her. If that still doesn't get you a call back, don't let too much time go by before you call management for help.

CHAPTER 2

Real Mentors Tell You:
Inspect, Don't Expect

Trust but verify

T rust is a beautiful thing. Your leadership team has entrusted you with a project and is counting on you to get it done. You already know that in order to build your credibility and be successful, you must execute. Whether you are the leader of a team, or simply a team member who will receive inputs from others (presumably inputs that you need in order to make your own commitments), you must ensure that others execute on their commitments to you, that they are on time and functioning at the desired quality level. You must not *expect* that other team members will do this, even if they *vow* they will.

In order to execute successfully, you must *inspect* the intentions, progress, methodology, and output of your colleagues. This is not to say that you should revert to pre-Peter Drucker-ian managerial practices when employees were treated with suspicion in terms of their desire, intent and ability to perform. Rather, a supportive ("testing" not "besting") environment of peer-review and mutual commitment to success should always be the order of the day. Employees who "inspect" don't have to respond to queries on their project status with the managerial equivalent of fingernails on a blackboard: phrases like "I think so," or, "that's what I was led to believe," or worse, "no one told me

> *The managerial equivalent of fingers on a blackboard: answers like "Nobody told me differently."*

differently" come to mind. Employees who inspect will **know**. Don't just expect or assume that timely or quality team deliverables will materialize. Make sure: ***inspect***.

To more fully understand the implications of "expecting" instead of "inspecting," imagine the two following scenarios:

Scenario 1:

Your team agrees to commit to a client that you will meet an emergency order of 2,000,000 more units of Product Awesome within two weeks. You, as leader, are able to make that commitment because representatives of each of the key business areas that will be contributing to the production of Product Awesome said they had adequate supplies or capacity to build the extra 2,000,000 units. However, four days before your team is due to ship the extra Product Awesome, the test team realizes that Product Awesome competes for test time with Product Outstanding and there are insufficient testers available to meet all of these test requirements. Suddenly, the team members realize they cannot possibly complete their regular commitments, much less send out the 2,000,000 extra units on time.

Scenario 2:

You need a contract reviewed by an Intellectual Property attorney before proceeding to the next phase of negotiations with a client. The IP attorney is unreachable but a legal assistant tells you that your particular document has been reviewed and it's O.K. for you to proceed with your next steps, based on the attorney's concurrence. You never confirm this yourself with the lawyer. After you have moved along, the assistant realizes that she made a mistake and calls to tell you that your legal eagle reviewed a different case, not yours. Having previously accepted her word, you have already made a now-inappropriate commitment to a client.

What happened and how could either of these negative outcomes have been avoided?

The inspection yardstick

You work with colleagues you have known for some time. You all get along and trust each other. This is terrific. Everyone should work under these conditions. However, if you are on the receiving end of commitments—and you depend upon the successful completion of those commitments to meet your own—you must make sure that colleagues and teammates who have made commitments to a project a) are actually empowered to make them, b) have done the homework necessary to make reliable commitments, c) have a valid approach to solving problems and making commitments, and finally d) are on track to keeping those commitments. If they don't meet their commitments then presumably you will have a hard time (or potentially impossible time) keeping yours, which will translate into delays and a lack of execution—for you.

Do not wait until your due date—or just before— to inspect.

As you meet or speak with members of your delivery team, listen carefully to their description of their own sub-team or individual progress. Are you hearing passive or active "speak?" If you hear passive, third-person commitments, as in "it was done" or "the task will be done," you should sense a potential for trouble and inspect. Take immediate corrective action, if necessary. Likewise, as you contribute to a team, you too should use an active, first-person voice. Ownership is what you need to model yourself and extract from others. Always insist on a firm, active commitment, both from yourself and from others: "*I* will do *this* task by *this* date."

31

Inspect vs expect: two aspects to consider

1. Organizational empowerment: Who is on the field?

As an individual member of a team, you will still count on others to perform some sub-segment of work that will in turn enable you to complete your work. When talking to these colleagues, you need to understand specifically *what* it is they will do and *when* they will do it, and if the task is not to be performed by them, *who* on their team will do it?

With that information in hand, follow up to assure that a) the individual is aware that he/she has been signed up to said task, which you are dependent on for your own success, and later, you must b) assure that the person in question is actually performing the task. Don't assume that the work is being performed, and by all means, do not wait until the due date, or just before the due date, to inspect. At the end of that day, no matter what has transpired or why, if you are late—at least from the perspective of your leadership team—it is you who did not deliver.

Looking back at our scenarios, in the instance of the legal assistant delivering verbal assurances, you would more than likely know not to proceed without having clarified your lawyer's position. And, to be fair, it is unlikely that a legal assistant would advise you to do so. Anyone who has spent any time with corporate lawyers knows that they hate to put anything unnecessary in writing. However, if you need their concurrence on anything, you'd better have it writing. But the imagined scenario is still useful because it brings up an important point: the person providing a commitment must be both empowered and appropriately placed in the organization. The greater the importance of the question at hand, the more important it will be

Inspect your data; your reviewer certainly will!

to speak directly to the mission owner and not to an intermediary, nor to anyone in a lesser position. My intention here is not to diminish those in lower level positions, but if the question at hand is mission-critical, wherein your manager (or someone else) is inspecting your data or your presentation—and there will always be someone inspecting your data and/or presentation—you may be asked, "You spoke to the CFO about this directly, and she said this?" You want your answer to be "yes." You do not want your answer to be, "No, I spoke to his assistant," or "I spoke to someone in one of his departments." Receiving such a response forces your reviewer/inspector to pick up the phone and call the CFO himself, and if he has to make that call to reassure himself that he understands the CFO's position, how does that help to build trust between the two of you? Do not hesitate to inspect. I have used a C-level managerial example here, but this notion of organizational appropriateness is relevant at all levels of a business. If the situation described in scenario one had actually happened, the "post-mortem" would surely have included an inspection of the commitments made by the test team. Was the real business unit owner (the test manager or leader) consulted? Or did you, our hero, accept a commitment and proceed without being assured that the person who made it was empowered to do so?

2. Input accuracy

> *"Never turn down a chance to look at data."*
> —*Dr. Tom Caulfield*

What if everyone agrees that a particular individual is performing a given task, has acknowledged delivery dates, and appears through regular reviews to be on schedule for completing the tasks on which you have a dependency. Is that enough? No. Because if the work is incomplete or incorrect, you are in the same position that you would have been had the work not been completed at all. Therefore, you must make it a practice to question the methodology used to gather and develop data or conclusions, and then carefully review the data that is being presented. Do the findings hang together with everything else you know? Do the developed data tables and graphs correspond to the reported raw data? Or, for example, in a presentation of findings, do the data on page seven agree with the summary on page twelve? Does the paperwork suggest that certain parts never went to test, yet upon closer inspection of cross-sectional X-rays of components, there is a clear indication of test probes? Does a sales pipeline include a client targeted to close $15M of business, while the client itself is only a $10M-sized firm? Do the results that you see defy physics? Ask to see any relevant data that supports a conclusion, especially if the conclusion does not line up with your expectation. Don't relegate your opinion to experts, but do talk to experts, even if the person delivering material is himself an expert. Peer review is a wonderful thing, and can strengthen the entire team if it is done in a non-combative, "let's-get-it-done-right-the-first-time," manner. Never take someone's data and run with it. Always perform some type of inspection.

Combining personal execution with personal inspection will set a very high standard of performance on a team.

Don't think of the practice of inspection as time-consuming or combative. It is a time-saving, winning device. Blind trust may yield an on-time, high-quality delivery, which would be great. However, if you inspect as you proceed, you can spot potential areas for trouble and fix them before they become show-stoppers.

It is fine, necessary, and indicative of good leadership to trust others to do the work that you need them to perform; however, it is risky to trust **blindly**. You must personally inspect for data integrity, thoroughness, project ownership, and commitment. Combining personal execution with personal inspection will set a very high standard of performance on a team, and will absolutely improve the odds of successful and on-time outcomes. As I entered the executive ranks at IBM, my manager's manager firmly warned me that while I would have many *opportunities* to make mistakes, his and the company's *tolerance* for mistakes would be very, very limited. This sobering note of caution reinforced the need to inspect information coming to me so that I could be certain that I was not passing on inaccurate or incomplete information to those above me. Inspecting, rather than expecting, also lends stability to the business, as the number of revisions or corrections that would be required from someone 'assuming' or 'expecting' things and later having to recant is vastly reduced. Perturbations impede trust, and we know that lack of trust impedes career success.

To be more successful and trustworthy, practice polite, professional inspection.

Mentoring Maxim

Real Mentors Tell You:
Listen to the Voices in Your Head

Andy Grove, former CEO of Intel Corporation, could not have been more on the mark when he coined the phrase "Only the Paranoid Survive", making his book title an enduring part of the corporate lexicon. Paranoia, I have learned from my mentors, contributes to execution excellence. Paranoia is your gut talking, and your gut is talking from experience. Listen carefully. Your gut will tell you if something is wrong. Pay attention to it, and go inspect.

- If a "little voice" in your head awakens you in the middle of the night over some small project detail, get up and verify that you have addressed it.

- If you are depending on something and/or someone and you have an inkling that that they are not really going to deliver, investigate.

- If you think that maybe some members of one of the sub-teams you are relying on didn't really answer all the questions put before them, or have perhaps overlooked something, explore that further.

- If you think person A could or should give you some valuable insight, and you haven't previously consulted person A, go consult.

- If you have any doubts about the team's overall ability to deliver, get help. Now.

It is critical to ask for help when there's smoke, not after there's a fire.

If in doubt about whether or not you should check on something, or bother to go the extra mile, ask yourself this question: If I don't do this thing I am thinking about, and this project fails, how will I explain it? Whenever I ask myself that question, I envision my manager's face, his manager's face, my colleagues' faces, and the "collective" face of my team. These "voices and visions" have prompted me to get out of bed many a night to confirm something or set up an investigation, or add to my "to do" list, because I'd rather execute now than explain later why I didn't.

Take it from me, when you need to execute, it's good to have and listen to the voices in your head.

Now that you are executing well and assuring everyone that you will deliver quality materials, how do you share this excellent news with the world? The answer: by being brief and to the point.

CHAPTER 3

Real Mentors Tell You:
If You Can't Net it, You Don't Know it

Be able to quickly and succinctly explain what has changed since the last time you met with an audience.

Start at the end!

Accountability and ownership are of course key parts of executing. Given that you "own" a project and assume responsibility for its success, you must be able to quickly and accurately explain what is going on with it. In articulating its status, you must be able to succinctly state if it is on schedule and budget, and if it's off, what you are doing about that and what help you need to get it back on schedule or budget. You always, always, always need to be able to explain what has changed with the project since the last time it was reviewed with a particular audience. All of this has to be explained clearly, with a minimum of digression and needless details.

Though not as important as **what** you say, **how** you say something and **how much** you say is also key. Verboseness is tiring and indicates that the speaker cannot cull out what's important. It is also potentially viewed with suspicion, as it can seem that the speaker (i.e., "explainer") is stalling or hiding behind a barrage of words, some of which may be useful, and under questioning, some that sound like a deflection. If your listener needs a decoder ring, a compass, and a suitcase in order to follow your thinking through a lengthy explanation, particularly on a not-too-complex topic, you are not netting well. Don't make your listener "work" for an answer, and don't waste "trust currency." If you can't summarize, you are not ready to meet your audience, and if you can't net, your audience will correctly conclude that if you can't net it, you don't know it.

Once more with conviction . . . and clarity and conciseness

Just as you are responsible for executing on your deliverables, you are responsible for advocating for them as well: on behalf of yourself, your project, your team, and your management chain. This means being able to 'sell' your project, get additional resources if you need them, and convey at all times that you are either under control or are quickly getting there. You should be readily able to answer questions about your deliverables, and that means no hedging or hesitation. Your audience will be listening for your level of conviction. You don't want to sound as if you yourself aren't convinced, even as you are trying to convince others. If you have been executing and inspecting, you should be convinced, right? Likewise, you should be able to articulate the big picture when that is the request, and avoid clouding that view with extraneous details and sidebars. You should also reserve the option of saying—occasionally—that you don't know an answer. I do mean occasionally, however, because if you frequently cannot respond to questions about your project or deliverables, then you clearly are not executing.

When you do respond to a query, as a minimum, just answer the question . . . or not.

We all *know* that if we don't know the answer to a question that we will not be summarily executed on the spot. If you are generally on top of matters, upon questioning it is perfectly acceptable to have to defer on one or two even compelling points. *We **know** this.*

Just answer the question . . . using just the facts.

42

But sometimes we forget ourselves. Sometimes, we may be on a roll and want to show that we know everything there is to know about our project. So we start talking, and talking . . . and talking. Sometimes, like politicians, there are subjects we have not been asked about, but we find them interesting, or we know a lot about them, or we think that they are important on some level—even if it's not necessarily the level we happen to be on—and we want to talk about them too. So we throw them in . . . and our audience is now taking an unanticipated journey far from the subject at hand.

Listening to a long-winded speaker irritates any time-constrained leader, yet they are often forced to endure an onslaught of words, which may or may not be useful in answering the most basic questions. If after a highly impressive, Emmy-worthy soliloquy, you are greeted with an impatient look and question, such as, "And so your answer is . . . ?" or, "I know there was an answer in there somewhere," you know that you are guilty (as we all have been) of not netting—and perhaps not knowing the subject thoroughly. This particular "vomiting phenomena" is most exasperating to the listener when it is accompanied by common and obvious "tells." The person attempting to respond to a question inadvertently signals that he or she really doesn't know the answer by speaking louder and faster as if to get it over with. He may look the listener right in the eye, not blink, widen his or her eyes, swallow hard, fidget, and throw in all manner of extraneous factoids and tangents. The answerer's strategy appears to be, "wear the listeners down with so many words that they are too irritated or bamboozled or time-constrained to ask additional questions." Another strategy appears to be, "If I don't know the actual answer, I'll just say everything I know about the topic and others here may know something and volunteer that and together, we or they will piece together an answer." After several

If you've admitted that you don't have the answers and have been given a reprieve, stop talking.

minutes of this, the answer is no clearer than when the conversation started.

What typically happens in these scenarios is that the time-constrained leader does run out of time and patience, and is left with a poor impression of the speaker. Or, the leader will *make time* to ask follow-up questions, usually in an attempt to get the speaker to link the previously listed factoids and tangents to the question at hand. This is not a positive scenario either, as even the most casual observer or time-constrained leader, along with everyone else in the room, realizes that the speaker is probably not very knowledgeable—at least not about the question on the table. If the line of questioning continues, matters can become uncomfortable as the tone of the questioning may grow more probing and insistent. This situation obviously needs to be avoided, as it once again impedes trust building. While you should always be prepared to address questions about a project, if you don't know an answer, simply admit it. Agree to follow up and come back (call or email or show up at the next meeting) with a correct answer. Once you have said you will come back with a more detailed response, stop talking. You have an exit—take it. If you continue speaking when it is apparent you are not prepared, you are needlessly hurting yourself.

If you know the answer, please reply succinctly. Please net!

Practicing netting

Netting is simply cutting to the chase. Before you make any presentation, before you go into a team meeting and before you write an email, look at your project status and develop essential talking points. Assume you have two minutes to tell your story. What is the most important message that you want to

> *Don't hold your audience in suspense: start your talk with the conclusion.*

convey? What is the essential message that you want everyone to take away from your discussion? What if you have five minutes or ten minutes—what more will you say?

At a minimum, your ideal, netted story will create a contrast between where you should be according to your plan versus where you are today, what has changed since the last time this audience heard from you, and what you plan to do next. If you need help, whether you have two minutes or twenty, make sure that gets an early mention. Also, never hold anyone in suspense, but tell them your "conclusion" right up front. Starting with a conclusion is a great way to demonstrate netting and to provide a framework for the rest of your talk or memo.

Net for your audience

The more senior the members of your audience, the more net your responses to questions should be. While I don't mean to imply that you should limit yourself to "yes" or "no" responses, please take note that very senior management will not be terribly interested in small details. Your immediate manager, on the other hand, will be. You should always have two to three key points to summarize and explain the rationale for your position. Always be prepared to articulate details, even if you haven't been asked to do so.

Communication protocol: net and clear.

These guidelines I've summarized for verbally responding to questions are applicable to other forms of communication as well.

Netted email, presentations, and you

If you are prepared to send or deliver an email or presentation, please assume that the audience for either is busy and inundated with other emails, calls that must be returned, and too many meetings on the calendar—not to mention their need to carve out some time to do "real" work. They probably have several other projects in the works, and the status of those must be retained in order for them to be able to guide or assist others, as well as explain to their own teams if asked. Your job is to make comprehending, retaining, and explaining your story easy for them, so be clear, be net, and start at the end. In developing any presentation or memo, you should keep these objectives in mind.

Writing an email or memo

If you **have** to write a memo (something I will question later), try to limit yourself to one or two sentences. In theory, you are attempting to inform, opine, or perhaps question—not have a persuasive argument. If you must send a lengthier email, please start with a short one-paragraph summary. You can label this short paragraph "summary," or our new favorite word, "net."

The "net" needs to provide readers with all project salient points, such that the reader won't need to read the second half of the memo, which should be labeled "details." Curiosity—and/or the desire to "inspect"—may lead readers to continue, but the content of your net should be sufficient for them to clearly understand your overall message.

By the way, in the "net" paragraph, the intent is not to develop the world's longest run-on sentence. Please keep it simple, because as we already know, if you can't net it, you don't know it. And if you don't know it, you definitely don't want to write it down! Your short email should simply include who, what, where, why and how, and any important implications associated with those points. State any problem you have encountered, if necessary, and describe who will handle the problem

> *Pick a descriptive email subject line. If you receive an email with an uninformative or vague subject line, change it before forwarding or replying.*

and when it will be solved. Before sending, read your missive again. If it isn't completely clear (i.e, the reader will have to follow up with you—not to take action yet, but to better understand you), start over.

Also, it's a fact of corporate life, long memos are either deleted without being read, or are skimmed before either being ignored or forwarded to someone else to handle. If you want to make sure that your missives are actually being read, write a note, not a book.

So now, let's go back to the question of, "Do you actually need to send an email?" We all get *a lot* of email: too much. While it's important that you inform others of what you are doing, or what you need, it is also important that you be judicious when using email.

If your manager is getting more email from you than from her entire leadership team, you are probably sending her too many. If your email is really intended to CYA (and we all know what that means), please reconsider sending them. Work on building trust. Go see the person you were intending to send an email.

Some email etiquette is warranted here:

> *Avoid the use of adverbs and adjectives. "A terrific increase" will drive requests to define "terrific" before any action is taken.*

1. **Choose an appropriate and succinct subject line.** This will save everyone time and help you get the responsiveness you need. Do not forward a previously titled email if it provides a now-poor description of the content of the email, or if you have chosen to address a different theme of the forwarded email. This is particularly relevant if the email relates to an important project. If an email is forwarded to you with a request for action, save everyone time by indicating your response in the title

line so that the reader knows the content of the email without having to actually open it. Simple descriptors like, "On it", "will close by 05/01," or "No Go" save everyone time. I can guarantee you that "No Go" will be opened. You should, of course, have a good net explanation for your "No Go" response.

2. **If a topic has generated a series of emails, stop.** Don't send another. Get everyone together for a 15-minute huddle and solve your problems.

3. **Avoid the use of adverbs and adjectives.** Instead, use quantitative descriptions. "Humongous increase in output," while descriptive, is not as informative as "75% increase in output." Using the quantitative description avoids unnecessary requests for follow-up action. Using 'humongous' for example, will invariably lead to a follow-up email or question asking, "What do you mean by 'humongous'?" That's wasting everyone's time.

4. **Limit the use of "bcc."(blind carbon copy).** There are a few good reasons to use "bcc," which means that few emails should require its use. Using the "bcc" to demonstrate to your manager that you are having an email argument with an opposing team member or colleague is not a credible reason for using it. Worse, don't use it with your manager's manager as a way of "sharing" your point of view in an email dispute with your own manager. It's that trust thing again.

Use "bcc" when you suspect that an issue will be surfaced to a higher level of management and you want that senior team briefed before the issue escalates. In that case, only use "bcc" if the senior team is familiar with the issue at hand. Otherwise, send a brief note summarizing the issue and advising of a pending escalation. If you are going to use the "bcc," note that its use should be limited to one to two levels of management or project leadership.

5. **Watch your tone and your messaging: get the reaction you intend.** Are you attempting to inform or incite? Are you trying to assure the reader or spur him to action? For example, don't state that something essential is under control, then conclude with a now—nullifying statement like, "Of course, nobody knows what Peter will do. We all know that he may throw a monkey wrench into this whole thing." Your reader will wonder if your project really is under control. If Peter is a wild card, you should have already spoken to Peter and closed with him before stipulating that your project was under control. Make sure your tone and your message is consistent throughout your email.

6. **Don't introduce tangential topics.** Stick to the topic in your subject line. An email is not like a phone call. Don't switch to a new topic while you "have your reader's attention."

7. **Resist the temptation to engage in email cage matches.** If someone sends you a blistering missive, or one that infuriates you with its blatant ignorance or hubris, don't start typing the equivalent of a molotov cocktail. Take an hour's break and afterward, consider picking up the phone and having a civil conversation with the other party. If that's not possible, try again tomorrow.

8. **If you need to discuss a sensitive topic, don't send an email.** In general, it is not a good idea to use emails to discuss sensitive topics. Face to face or by phone is the only way to handle sensitive topics.

9. **Don't send an email if any portion of your note will contain the sentence, "I am sorry to send this to you via email."**

Figure 1 below, Memo Mojo, provides a useful summary.

Memo Mojo

- **Set up the response. Why are you writing this memo?**
  Context is key, so don't just start writing.
- **Answer the question—and only the question.**
  Start with the answer, and don't introduce new topics.
- **Be very net, and very clear.**
  More than two paragraphs are not likely to be read. Provide details as an attachment, or specify that details follow the summary of your email. This gives the reader the option to stop at the summary, or continue reading to inspect the details.
- **When referring to a project status, structure responses relative to the plan.**
  You do need to have a plan, and you should acknowledge that your status in on/better than/or worse than plan.
- **If next steps are appropriate, use action-oriented language.**
  Don't 'hope', 'wish' or 'be waiting for' something to happen. Instead, identify what you will do to make it happen.
- **Lean on facts and data: don't opine or use too many adjectives.**
  Avoid: "That will never happen" or "Everything is absolutely terrific." "I foresee a major disconnect." "We had humongous yield losses."
- **Be mindful of your tone: pick a theme and stick to it.**
  You can't assert that you are on track in one sentence and refute it in another.
- **Pick a descriptive topic or headline for your memo.**
  Don't merely forward an email that has a no-longer relevant title, or one that was never descriptive in the first place.
- **If you are answering an email in which you were requested to act, acknowledge that in the title of your response.**
  A simple, "Got it", "On it", or "Acknowledged, back in two days" respects your reader's time and will be appreciated.
- **If you want your reader to act immediately, please specify that in your title.**
  A "Your Action Required" headline is appropriate if you need someone to do something and no real urgency is required. Conversely, "Ringing the Bell" will capture attention and signal a need for immediate reaction.

Figure 1: Memo Mojo

With respect to developing presentations, similar rules apply.

Presentation prowess

From my perspective, the first two rules of effective presentation are: eliminate suspense and start by creating a 'frame' or structure for the story you are about to tell. Do not force your audience to take a journey with you through 30 slides before they discover what your intentions are, or what you are recommending. Also, make sure you really need those 30 slides. Most people find more than 15 slides to be tiresome. Even if you have one-half hour allotted to you on the agenda, make sure you have a summary that allows you to 'message' if you only get two minutes to speak. Because meetings typically cover several agenda topics, and also because our colleagues may run over during their allocated time slots, a presenter can never be sure that there will be adequate time (or the allotted time) to conduct a thorough review of his topic.

Inspire us, don't retire us.

You can always be invited back or otherwise schedule follow-up time with pertinent leaders; in the meantime, be prepared to make good use of the available time—no matter how short—by having a good conclusions chart to start, and a few supporting charts. Be ready to offer to deliver your presentation in whatever small increment of time the audience has available. Your objective in making an internal presentation (i.e., not a sales presentation to a client) is to get "on stage" and deliver your easily understood message—no matter how complex the topic—and get "off stage." While "on stage", you want to project your "I will achieve or exceed the plan" persona. If your message is not that positive, then your aim is to convince everyone that you are that same winner who will quickly get back on plan. Then you want to get off the stage. If you are stuck on stage, one of the following must apply: you can't net, you don't have a solid proposal, or you aren't executing well and now have some explaining to do—all cases to be avoided.

Just as are there are a few rules of the road for emails, there is a guide for presentations as well:

1. **Don't start your talk with a slide.** Before you put one slide on the overhead or screen, please introduce yourself, your topic, and your conclusion. Your audience should know what your slides will address before they see them. In this way, you are focusing their attention on **why** you've drawn the conclusions you have. This overview is your best project-selling tool as it sets you up for a successful presentation—or not.

2. **Start with a bang—and recover from the introduction if necessary.** If you and your topic have already been introduced by the session host or the previous presenter, don't merely repeat, "As John said, I'm Jane Doe and I am here to talk about Project Awesome." It's much more interesting, after acknowledging the person who introduced you, to start right away with your summary; i.e., "The last time we looked at this, Project Awesome was off schedule. Today you'll see that we are back on track and prepared to deliver to the budget right on time." Now you have everyone's attention, and appropriately, in full inspection mode, their attention will be focused on what you have done, and why you are back on schedule. Even if your story is not positive, you should still do this, as you will need to direct everyone's attention to where you need help and why. If you do need help, make sure to include that fact in your summary.

> *Start your talk with a compelling statement, not "As John said, I'm Jane Doe and I'm here to talk about what John just said I'm here to talk about."*

53

In this latter case, your start should go something like this, "The last time we reviewed Project Awesome, we were off schedule by one month. Today, while we will see some improvement, you will note that we have not fully recovered to the plan. While we know how to get back on track, which I will discuss in the next fifteen minutes, Part C is still problematic due to these three factors (followed by a brief list) and I will need your help to close at least one of those three things." Since resources are scarce in most organizations, you will want to briefly acknowledge that there are implications to assigning you the now unplanned resources that you are requesting, and state that you will address these implications in your talk. Only then are you ready to proceed with your first slide.

3. **Inspire us, don't retire us.** Too many charts, too many words, too many word charts, a lack of color—in the slides and in your delivery—all these add up to dull presentations. Unless you are a marketing or sales whiz addressing clients, keep it simple, active, and as short as you can.

4. **Tell us why we care—immediately.** Don't simply show a list of activities completed and expect that your audience will appreciate them. Please explain immediately what _benefit_ the business derives as a result of you and/or your team achieving these milestones or events.

5. **Focus on content, not imagery.** Unnecessary or inappropriate use of icons or imported images to fill or dress up slides can be distracting in a presentation. If the basic content of your presentation is lacking, or you are off the plan

pace for any reason, *and* you have these extraneous images throughout your presentation, you risk leaving the impression that rather than working to improve your project status, you've invested time in finding obscure images or dressing up your slides. Also, even if you are on the plan pace but you have 'dressed up' your presentation with images that increase the size of your presentation (i.e., your five slide presentation deck is 10MB because it's loaded with unnecessary images), you risk alienating your audience. Unless you are preparing a marketing or sales deck for a client presentation, leave the 'gee-whiz' kit in the drawer.

6. **Don't put anything on a slide that you can't thoroughly explain.** Meeting with team members who have given you input is part of your preparation. If, under questioning during your presentation, you have to say one time too many, that you "Got that data from Joe, and need to check with him to clarify", you will undermine all of the credibility you've established. If you can't explain it, it doesn't belong in your slides. *And* if it belongs on your slides, don't simply delete it because you can't explain it: go research the answers you need. If it's D-Day and you don't have those answers, you can optionally include the topic in the slides, and indicate that you are still working on this angle.

7. **Don't keep looking back at your slides or read them to the audience.** You know what you are going to say, don't you? You should be able to stand off to the side and/or in front of the screen while talking without looking back. You should be able to advance your slides, keep talking and not look back because you know what's on them. You can refer to the slides when

you want to emphasize something important. You should have additional information to discuss that's not on your charts, but that additional information should be introduced only when you are on the slide that covers that particular topic. Otherwise, the audience concentration will be diluted as they look back and forth between you and your slides, trying to decide where to focus.

8. **And now a word from your posture.** You have heard about your posture before, probably from your mother. During an office presentation, if you stand in one place, rigid or slumped over, arms crossed, you risk looking afraid or not at all confident or sure about your message. Stand up straight, move away from the screen, make eye contact, have *some* animation. A presentation is not a dreaded obligation, but rather an opportunity—a necessary opportunity—to inform and sell. So sell.

9. **Know when to stop.** When delivering your pitch, please pay attention to the "hook." If you are effectively being told that your pitch is over (I.e., "I got the chart.", "I read the rest of the slides.", "I got it.", "We saw the same story yesterday." or something similar), don't insist. If you have something critical to discuss and you haven't gotten to that yet, simply clarify, and assert that you want to be sure that everyone is aware of "X" before you stop. If they are, stop. To continue is to risk annoying your audience. You are done. You put a lot of work into your charts and you want to show them. Do yourself a favor, though—if you hear the hook, fall out of love with your charts. Do not try to squeeze whatever remains of your chart deck into 30

If you get the 'hook', fall out of love with your slides. Stop talking. Sit down.

seconds. Your next three moves are very simple: listen, stop, sit down.

10. **If you are presenting via teleconference, take a breath!** Understand that there is a central conference room somewhere (wherever the final decision maker or approver happens to be sitting). Start your talk by summarizing, then pause for a reaction from the folks on the phone. Ask if there are questions about your summary. If not, proceed. Always talk in short "bursts," and frequently check in with listeners to allow for input. This is essential: make sure you allow listeners to interject questions. Not allowing "interruptions," or talking over those who try to ask questions will merely frustrate your audience, and ruin a potentially good presentation. If there are no questions, ask one—if only to assure that your listeners are still engaged. Many of your colleagues listening in will be armed with mute buttons and laptops, so if you drone on without ensuring that your audience is engaged, they may opt to do other things—like attend to that pile of email. Since you cannot see them, checking in with them is the best way to get interim feedback.

11. **If you can't make your presentation but have to submit slides, make sure they can stand alone.** In other words, make sure their message is clear and net.

12. **Be prepared for electronic or audience failure.** What if your laptop dies? What if there's no overhead projector—or its bulb is out? What if there are no calamities, but you sense that your audience is tired and isn't terribly interested in another stack of charts? Always be prepared to make a presentation

without your slides. If you've practiced netting, you should be able to discuss your topic unassisted by visual aids. They are "aids" after all—and not essential. Don't allow yourself to be hamstrung by technology failures.

Finally, you know you need to be prepared. In addition to delivering the message you want to deliver, you should look over your presentation and prepare yourself to answer any questions the audience might ask: perhaps something that someone *not* in the forest might wonder about. Which brings us to our next topic . . .

CHAPTER 4

Real Mentors Tell You:
Anticipate the Obvious

What's everybody looking at?

Whether you are writing a memo, giving a presentation, or simply talking about your project, you are at all times advocating for its success as well as and your own. You know to prepare to answer the usual questions about your project—"How's it going?", "Are you on time and/or on budget?", etc.—and you should be able to answer these in your sleep. However, there are other questions that your leadership team or audience will think are obvious, and you should know how to anticipate and answer them quite readily as well.

You have the very best intentions when you make a presentation. You have spent time preparing your remarks and have developed clear talking points in support of the message you want to convey. However, even with that, you should also take a second or third pass over your presentation to determine what others who are less involved (i.e., those not in the forest) may see, then prepare yourself to answer any questions that might arise from the "vision" they may form when listening to your pitch. Following are a list of questions which you should always anticipate getting. Do not plan to give a talk without having prepared net answers to these questions:

1. What has changed since the last time we reviewed this project?

2. If any data point looks markedly different from most of the other data points, what is causing that difference?

3. Page to page or paragraph to paragraph, is the story you are telling consistent? I.e., does the data on page seven match the data on page nine?

4. If you are off schedule, do you need any help? (There is a "correct" answer to this question, by the way.)

5. Does any math you've used add up properly?

6. If you are off schedule and over budget (or under, in either case), how did that happen?

7. What do you think will happen next? What are you doing to stop that or, how do you plan to expedite that action (whichever is pertinent)?

8. What can we (you) do better next time?

As an example, take a look at Figure two, below. Try to guess what questions would be asked of anyone presenting the data in Figure two.

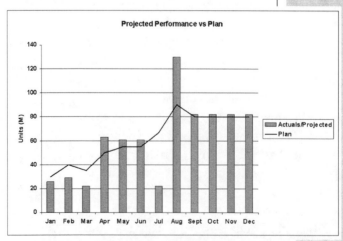

Figure 2: Projected Performance vs Plan

Did you guess:

1. Why is the monthly performance so erratic?

2. Is the plan competitive or commensurate with the industry?

3. Why are you off the plan in 1Q and 3Q?

4. What's going on in March, and more particularly, in July, such that you're so far off plan?

5. How much money or market share are we losing because you are off plan?

6. What are you doing to get back on plan?

7. What do you need from us to go faster?

8. Who has been tagged to help you?

9. What's causing the plan to grow so dramatically up through August? Why does it taper off and plateau after?

10. Why does performance also remain flat from September through 4Q?

11. What's going to happen in April, May and June that will guarantee that you will achieve your plan? Why can't that happen January thru March?

12. What has changed since the last time we looked at this? Is performance getting better or worse? Why?

13. What can you do to exceed the plan?

14. What is supposed to happen between June and August to get that kind of growth?

15. Why is August the peak month? Why does performance retreat in September?

16. Can you pull some of that August performance into July for smoother performance over 3Q?

For those of you who are astute enough to have approximated the average performance over the year versus the average planned performance over the year, you know that the two averages are the same. However, while it is true that on a full-year basis, someone putting up this kind of performance will have achieved his or her full-year target, it must be highlighted that this same person will have performed poorly in the first quarter, exceeded the plan in the second quarter, gone into the dog house in July, and by the third quarter, no one would have known what to expect from him or her. To be evaluated as a high performer, consistency—that is consistent execution and delivery—is essential and very much appreciated. Achieving what you told the business you would achieve—as a minimum—and delivering on the date and budget you told them to expect it, is essential for success.

> *"Consistency is better than precision."*
> —*Kevin Kenlan*

In anticipating the obvious, whatever you do, know what you said the previous time you met with a review team, because if you've done a good, clear job of netting, your audience will remember. In any new communication, they will be looking for signs of progress or less impressively, lack thereof. This is especially true when you are conveying information on critical projects or key business metrics. Leaders will have found some mnemonic or other means of remembering your data (i.e. "I am sure that you said $1981M because I remember thinking that 1981 was the year I joined this company!") With that, you must always level-set your audience: start out at the point where you left them. Avoid:

- changing analysis methodology or base assumptions more than once during your project, and only then if absolutely necessary. If your base is not stable, then the audience cannot determine if your project is under control or not.

- inconsistent rounding, both in line item detail as well as in any totals.

- making significant changes to the format of any routine presentation. You don't want your audience to have to continuously work to understand your 'flavor of the week' format. Instead, you want them to focus on your results. Prefer to add information and clarity without making constant and dramatic format changes.

To help you make the most of presenting data and presenting yourself, in the next chapter we will explore the importance of choosing the right words to describe yourself and your intentions.

CHAPTER 5

Real Mentors Tell You:
The Verb's the Thing

Say—and do—what you mean

We all know that we don't get a second chance to make a good first impression. As you make your way through your career, you want to make sure that everyone you come into contact with knows that you have put *yourself* on a path to excel. You will start down this path anew each year when you develop your annual business commitments to your organization. You will be measured on these commitments, not only at the end of the year, but also, and as importantly, in each interaction that you have with your colleagues and leaders. It is for this reason that you must reach for and act according to 'leadership language'—avoiding 'languish language' at all costs.

Languish language contains verbs that signal lethargy and lack of ownership. These words indicate that the employee who uses them and acts on them is signing up to deliver little and puts himself or herself justifiably at risk to receive a poor annual performance appraisal. Typical languish language verbs include: '*support*', '*participate*', '*monitor*', '*track*', and '*assist*'. Most employees don't intend to project convey such an unengaged, lethargic impression of themselves, but these words mindlessly and unfailingly appear in conversations, presentations, emails, and annual commitment documents. Prized employees use, act on, and are rewarded for leadership language. This language includes verbs such as: *'develop'*, *'manage'*, *'execute'*, *'deliver'*, *'solve'*, *'invent'*, *'innovate'*, *'collaborate'*, etc.

In theory, an employee is reading his annual commitment plan several times a year. During this personal review process, the employee must ask himself if in fact he is doing—as a minimum—everything he signed up to deliver. It is easy to answer "Yes" if one has only signed up to 'track' or 'monitor', but how has tracking or monitoring moved the business forward? Further, when you read the chapter on "SWOT—Knowing your Competition", you'll know that you don't want to be and can't afford to be in the "track" or "monitor" camp. If you are using leadership language and more importantly, acting on it, you will have clearly moved the business forward, and that will be reflected in your annual evaluation, as well as in the growth opportunities that will come your way.

> *"I hear you talking but I want to see what you can <u>do</u>."*
> —*Fred Glasgow*

Use leadership language in your annual commitment plan, in your career development plan, and in all your interactions with others. Walk the talk, and stimulate your management team to evaluate your performance in those same terms. Everybody wins.

—RMTYT—

Nobody appreciates a hot air bag. We all understand that words are just that, mere words. However, the words you choose to describe yourself and your actions will be used by your peers and managers to formulate an opinion of you, your sense of urgency and your level of engagement. Take advantage of this penchant, and always project a leadership 'you'. Make every interaction count. This chapter addresses choosing the appropriate language for a leader—language that gives the impression that our reader is a 'do-er' and should be given the opportunity to 'do'. The wrong choice of verb in describing oneself, for example, can lead to the opposite effect. You can quickly be judged as a "side line player" and not even be offered the opportunity to 'do' or 'lead'. It's important to watch what you say, say what you mean, then do what you say.

Let's look at some examples:

Bob is asked where he is on Project Awesome. Bob shows his milestone chart, and while most of his early items are coded as 'complete', an upcoming milestone is coded 'yellow' or 'red,' indicating that Bob is at risk for not being able to hold the project schedule. When asked what is stopping him from proceeding on schedule, Bob replies, "I am waiting for Barbara to finish task B and deliver the data I need."

At senior levels of any business, I can assure the reader that such a response will be greeted with some degree of impatience and incredulence. Responses like these are not generally well-received. One could reasonably expect a protracted silence and an eventual response—even said gently—similar to,

"Waiting? You are waiting? And are we are all waiting with you? Is that our plan, to wait?"

One should never be *merely waiting* for anything. Never let such a passive phrase escape your lips. The

Waiting is generally not a good strategy for success.

leader to whom you are making this statement—after having mentally characterized *you* as someone who has time to '*wait*', and after having recovered from the shock that you clearly do not comprehend the proper urgency of the project you have been entrusted with—will now simply lead you down the path of steps which you must take in order to get your particular roadblock erased. By the way, dear reader, please also note that the words "hope" and "wish" are also found in this same passive category. Unless you work for a religious organization, "hope" is not an action word and is never appropriate. "Working" is entirely preferable to "wishing." Engaged, active people make things happen, they don't hope, wish, or wait for their arrival.

So what should you say when you need someone else to deliver something in order to complete your own tasks? A thorough—and active—person who wants to **demonstrate** that she is handling the task at hand, would say something like the following:

"I need B data from Barbara, which Barbara committed for delivery on Monday. Monday is late, so I've asked Barbara to sign-up to deliver on Friday, which while still not optimal, would allow us to hold the overall schedule. Barbara is reviewing this request with her team and will get back to me tonight. So, for the moment, I am showing the status as 'yellow' until I close this item with Barbara—tonight."

And what response from the leader might you anticipate if you provide such an answer?

"Let me know if you need help."

You'll get this kind of desirable response because you're demonstrating that you understand what needs to be done and you are executing. Waiting, wishing, and hoping will also get you 'help' and 'inspection', but probably not the kind that you'll enjoy. Choose your words carefully to get the 'help' and 'attention' that you want and need, when you want and need it. Let's examine leadership language in the context of annual commitments.

Annual performance commitments and reviews

While the example above referred to a project review, the lesson is equally valid in the context of describing your annual business commitments. Of course, you want to align your personal contribution goals with those of the organization. To have orthogonal goals—even good and lofty ones—will not necessarily be rewarding (well, not financially and career-wise). Equally as important as the alignment of goals with the business at hand, is to create your goals with a desired performance level score in mind. For example, if you want to receive a high mark at your annual performance review, and along with that, receive greater financial rewards and greater opportunities to expand your career, you are going to need to use and perform to active, leadership words. Conversely, if you are willing to receive fewer rewards, or no rewards (and who wants that?), choose passive words, act on them, and you can pretty much guarantee yourself that you will not have a very rewarding year. You will also risk giving the impression of yourself as a passionless person with little ownership for tasks assigned to you or expected of you. This is very easily avoided by using leadership language, and by performing accordingly.

Leadership language

The list below is representative of the only types of verbs you should use to describe the work you are doing, particularly if you are a senior level staff member. If you don't have an assignment that allows for the honest use of these verbs, it is very likely that, as a senior level employee, you are not thought of as a high-performance team member. If you are a relatively inexperienced employee, work towards procuring assignments that will allow you to accurately use these words to describe your mission. The more senior an employee you are or want to be, the more this leadership language applies to you.

Figure three provides some examples of leadership language.

Leadership Language			
Improve	Augment	Cost-Reduce	Exceed
Integrate	Invent	Guide	Devise
Develop	Lead	Structure	Establish
Direct	Influence	Design	Architect
Initiate	Build	Construct	Mentor
Aggregate	Synthesize	Form	Grow
Pioneer	Cultivate	Advance	Strengthen
Promote	Foster	Consult	Expand
Deliver	Collaborate	Create	Manage

Figure 3: Leadership Language

Languish language

Finally, just as there is language that connotes a 'can do' spirit, there is also a language of 'by-standers'. This kind of language incorporates words which are likely to net our reader a poorly perceived professional persona and poor annual review results, mainly because use of passive verbs do not indicate even any intent to lead. The person using this language is classifying himself as a "helper," and clearly abdicates his share of greater rewards and respect.

Figure four provides some typical languish language.

Languish Language			
Coordinate	Interface	Join	Organize
Support	Arrange	Adminster	Strive
Try	Aide	Watch	Monitor
Observe	Track	Handle	Help
Assist	Participate	Hope	Wish

Figure 4: Languish Language

Needless to say, we can't invent or advise on all fronts. Today, we all have to multi-task and will not necessarily lead all projects in which we are involved. That being said, it is certainly fine to see *moderate* use of "enabling" language instead of leadership language. However, this language should not be prevalent in any document or speech you prepare, nor should it predominate in any stance you take.

Finally, there is no question that leadership language alone is insufficient for personal success. Changing your vocabulary allows you to 'transmit' to others what you think you are capable of, as well as indicate the high level of performance output you plan to deliver. It causes others to look at you, at least initially, through that lens. Without question though, in order to be successful, this leadership vocabulary must be realized with thorough execution. As you review your presentation techniques, personal career development plans and annual performance commitment plan—and you do review that document several times a year, don't you?—make sure you are living up to "leadership language," not "languish language." If it's broke, fix it.

CHAPTER 6

Real Mentors Tell You:
There's an Art to Arguing

Office karate

The pressure at work can sometimes get the best of any of us. Perhaps a colleague or manager is having a bad day. The guy down the hall gets under your skin every time he opens his mouth. There is a critic in every crowd. Some people are just jerks. Sometimes though, they are not jerks, but are frustrated over whatever is happening (or not happening) in their own worlds at the moment. Sometimes people lose their cool. Despite any negativity, you need to maintain your composure at all times in the office if you want to be successful. There is an acceptable way to disagree with or 'engage' (AKA 'argue with' in the world outside of the office) peers in the office, and particularly in public forums. Even if you are not inclined to be argumentative, you should understand when you are being 'engaged', and learn how to react accordingly.

> *"To win, we need everybody on the team to play their roles, and play them well."*
>
> —*Michael J. Cadigan*

Part of having a 'winning' culture is to accept the notion of 'inspection', which as we know by now, is the reasonable review of intent, methodology, consistency, and results. Sometimes the tone of an inspection can become challenging, particularly when an idea being put forth seems ill-considered, or the presenter otherwise appears ill-prepared.

The following are examples of acceptable and typical phraseology for office "challenges." If you hear a few of these directed your way, it is likely that your data is being inspected, which we all agree is perfectly acceptable. However, if several of the comments below are directed your way, eventually combined with an unmistakably direct and frustrated tone, you are being "engaged":

1. "Perhaps I misunderstood you, I thought you said earlier . . ."

2. "Let me see if I understand what you are saying.", and what you hear back is not that clear.

3. "I distinctly heard you say 'no' before. Are you saying "yes" now"?

4. "I believe that page seven of your pitch said that item was 'late,' not 'on time' the way this page does."

5. "I spoke to Bob last night and what you are saying here is not consistent what he said."

6. "Have you ever seen that kind of success (or ramp, etc) happen **before** this mind-blowing, amazing project?"

7. "Why should we believe that this will work?"

8. "And whose idea was that?"

9. "Why would anyone do that?"

10. "Tell me again why (or how) you interpreted the data like that?"

> *When you are being engaged, slow it down, don't ramp it up.*

11. "I'd like to understand what you're saying, but I just don't."

12. "Maybe somebody *else* in the room can explain your logic to me . . ."

Grace under fire . . . and while firing

If any of these remarks are directed at you, perhaps followed by a prolonged, wordless stare, immediately clarify, remembering to always speak in "net" as much as possible. You should be polite and answer factually—never defensively. If several of these comments are launched, the atmosphere can get tense. The best defense under these kinds of verbal challenges is a cool head and solid, net answers. Absolutely the worst thing you can do is lose your temper and fire back. Even if you answer well and get everyone 'back in the box', you'll present yourself as 'emotional' or 'irrational' if you come out with guns blazing. You'll look 'out of control' even though you've been 'simply asked about your project'.

> *There is a professional way to disagree with and even challenge others.*

If the shoe is on the other foot, and it is you who would like to 'engage' a peer, some of the above expressions may be suitable. Always avoid insulting or talking down to your colleagues. Even as we "argue" in the office, we should always allow our peers a graceful stage exit. Humiliation has no place in the modern office. It's fine to convey to someone that his or her message is either not acceptable or is convoluted, but telling them that does not require 'attitude' or sarcasm. Whether in response to being challenged, or when challenging others, don't allow yourself to be made to look irrational—look 'net'.

If you disagree with a presented trail of logic and you'd prefer to avoid a confrontation, there is a professional way to disagree with others that should not cause them to see 'red'. The following examples politely express a countering opinion, while at the same time encourage additional discussion:

1. "Let me tell you why I see it differently." Or, "Can I tell you why I see it differently?" also works.

2. "While I understand all of that, I also think, however . . ."

3. "I don't agree with your conclusion, because . . ."

4. "Well, here are my thoughts."

5. "This is what I would've done, given what I've heard/seen here today."

6. "Did you consider any of the following?", followed by a list of options.

7. "I'm not sure I agree."

8. "I agree with you but" . . . followed by suggestions along an entirely different path.

These options do not generally lend themselves to the creation of a firestorm. If you do wind up in a heated exchange, do allow the opposing party a graceful exit, out of the argument or out of the room. You don't have to agree with everyone, nor does everyone have to agree with you. You do need to agree on a course of action (next steps) to resolve whatever it is you disagree on before you end your encounter. Let it go when you leave. You will likely have to work with your colleague again, AND you don't have to *smite* anyone just because you happen to be right.

When to speak up, when to shut up

There are going to be times when you are going to need to enter a fray and there are times when it's best to stay out of one. When in doubt as to whether or not it is appropriate to opine, please note that there are at least two ways to address this burning question: organizationally and personally.

"You can't be an engineer and NOT have an opinion."
—Dr Tom Caulfield

- If by virtue of your role in the organization you 'should' have an opinion, speak up. In other words, if the discussion topic is on 'cooling semiconductor devices' and you are the division's leading thermal design engineer, you are expected to have an opinion. In this case, because organizationally you are expected to have an opinion, you *need* to speak up. This is not the time to look down at your shoes.

- If a peer in your organization beats you to the punch and offers up an opinion similar to the one that you would have given, it is okay to say simply, "I agree." You can stop there.

- If a peer in your organization beats you to the punch and offers up an opinion that is different from the one that you would give, a response like, "I see it differently, and for the following reasons," is appropriate. Please briefly list your reasons and allow the discussion to proceed naturally.

- If you think that that a good solution that has been put forth but is being ignored, and you have the expertise or formal ability to validate or support that solution, by all means, speak up. If you have no such expertise, but your gut tells you that something key is being ignored, speak up and ask to have a subject matter expert weigh in.

- If you have no formal role, but feel that you have a realistic option that could be helpful and this option has not yet surfaced, then by all means, speak up.

- You should shut-up when you are not following the conversation well (or are behind, or have come in late, etc), or you are not completely sure about the relevant facts or the integration thereof, or you have no organizational knowledge of the issues at hand and relatedly, don't understand the implications of any decision taken. This means that if the accountants are arguing over an obscure accounting ruling and you are an engineer with no accounting knowledge (i.e., no organizational knowledge), you should probably not interject a strong opinion (you are unlikely to understand generally accepted accounting principles or protocols or rationales for decisions or points of view).

- You should refrain from "seconding" the opinion of even an expert, if you have no real subject knowledge yourself. You are likely present because you have other contributions to make.

- You should be silent whenever your team is making a presentation and you are not the previously agreed-upon presenter. This is important. If you are not 'on stage', then please be a member of the listening audience. If the presenter needs help from someone in attendance, allow them to ask for help. If you are asked to respond, be brief, positive, generally supportive of the speaker, and hand the floor back over to the speaker as quickly as possible.

- If you have not been asked for help, but disagree with what the speaker has said—and have a reasonable idea or opinion—you should bring it up in such a way that the speaker (and the credibility of the work to date) is not thwarted (i.e., say "John highlighted the primary path we are exploring. Another path we are going to take a look at is . . ." Or, "another path worth exploring is", then briefly (in one or two sentences) state your idea. Conclude with a wrap-up like, "So, a little more work to be done on this front," then hand the floor back over to the speaker. This gives the speaker the option to gracefully acknowledge the idea and move on. You should not surface your idea if it's entirely new to your team, unless you preface your comments with that warning. Note that too many instances of 'new, last minute' ideas from you that crop up while someone else is presenting will not be appreciated by your colleagues or team.

- If you disagree with what the speaker has said, but your issue is not really substantive, let it go. To bring up a minor disagreement is only disruptive. You can always follow up with the speaker later. Generally, the time to discuss projects with your peers is before presentations or management review. Do your work off-line, not in the general manager's conference room.

- Did you get a big raise? A terrific bonus? A wonderful performance evaluation? A not so good performance evaluation? Call your mom—she will enjoy and appreciate hearing from you. The folks in the office? Not so much. There is not a lot of upside for you in sharing this kind of information in the office.

- Finally, you should shut up in reaction to 'the squeeze'. The squeeze is a 'ploy' used to question a speaker who is not quite getting the job done. The speaker may be stumbling just a bit—perhaps not being clear enough, or perhaps having some minor contradictions. The listener or worse, *listeners*, noting the contradictions or lack of clarity starts to ask more probing questions. The speaker becomes rattled. At this point, the speaker has two options: 1) stop talking after conceding that there are contradictions that need to be cleared up before proceeding further, or 2) collapse under the pressure of the squeeze and spill his guts. When speakers start to spill, usually it's a big spill—names, dates, places, etc. Obviously, the first choice above—concede and shut up—is the better and more graceful approach to dealing with the squeeze.

The Special Occasions

Shadow programs

If you have been are invited to 'shadow' (spend time with a senior employee to observe how he functions), pay attention, and unless otherwise directed, ask questions discretely to prevent disrupting the flow of normal meetings or appointments. If you must attend to your own normal activities, step away and take care of them. When you return to your shadow session, you should be completely engaged in what is going on there. If you are 'present', your host will take time to explain important points to you either then or later during your time together. Your host will notice if you are uninvolved or bored.

Checking emails is a sure sign of boredom and lack of engagement. Showing more interest in doing your email than attending to the business you are in theory learning about, will further give the impression that you have valued neither the shadow experience nor your host's time.

VIP visits

If you are invited to attend a briefing session, or to a 'meet and greet' with a visiting (or local) VIP, this is the time to have something *generally positive* to say. VIPs are usually quite interested in hearing an unfiltered view of what the 'regular' folks are thinking, so along with good news, it's also fine and desirable to discuss issues if they are problematic and within the power of the VIP to fix. It is also useful, and makes a very positive impression, if you have some reasonable, rational, and cost-effective ideas for fixing the problem. This is not the time to 'leak', ceaselessly complain, gossip, make accusations, or monopolize the conversation. Your peers have also come to listen and learn something from the VIP, after all. Brevity, a positive attitude, and a discernable desire to be helpful will likely get you future 'meet and greet' invitations.

VIP "meet and greet" sessions provide an occasion to briefly volunteer generally positive and entirely factual information.

Hosted dinner or lunch meetings

If you are invited to an assigned seating dinner or luncheon at which several VIPs are in attendance and act as table hosts, once you are seated, remain at your table for the duration of the event. Do not get up to visit other tables or introduce yourself to other table VIPs. Save this networking for the conclusion of the event. If you leave the table to visit other tables, you indicate a lack of interest or respect for your table host. For these kinds of events, you are a 'working' guest. Stay at your table and do your share of upholding the conversation.

Mentoring Maxim

Real Mentors Tell You:
Don't Blow Shadowing Opportunities

I have seen employees snag desirable job offers following a week of shadowing, and I've seen employees completely blow career opportunities and opportunities to expand their networks. If you are offered a shadowing opportunity, take it and leave your email and other daily tasks behind for a significant portion of the workday! If you are in the middle of a critical project at work, and you cannot afford to dedicate a significant portion of your attention to your host and his activities, reschedule the shadow date. You cannot learn from your host nor get into the 'flow' of your host's business if you are constantly going back to your normal job activities.

Shadow programs should be taken seriously, and attendees need to be interested and engaged. If a shadower cannot muster up enough interest and enthusiasm during the short shadowing program, a subsequent mentoring arrangement or job offer is unlikely. Don't waste these opportunities.

CHAPTER 7

Real Mentors Tell You: Collaborate to Win

There's always an expert around when you need one

We are all familiar with the old adage, "There's no 'I' in the word team." While there is always room for individual excellence, in the broader corporate world the best solutions often are derived from multiple points of view. It is rare to find that a solution put forth by an individual is as as well thought-out and solid as one put forth by a high-performance team. No one is expected to arrive at optimum decisions or create breakthrough products alone.

With that in mind, note that not only is it OK to seek input from experts, or those in the know who are not necessarily on your team, it is even advisable. Receiving expert input will further your cause when it comes to to executing well. Without expert input, you can potentially introduce project delays as stumbles or miscalculations can send you back to the 'fact finding' or 'discovery' phase of a project. It is in your best interests to know experts, or know how to find experts, in fields that are important in your current assignment. Knowing them is a big help; knowing how to work with them will take you further.

> *"To be successful, you need to respect and be able to work with everyone—up the chain, down the chain, and across the chain."*
> —*John DiToro*

You already know that you don't want to burn any bridges. In the corporate world, people come and go—intra-departmental and divisional transfers are common—and then they sometimes return. Or, they are placed in positions from which they can either help you someday, or forget you are alive. You can help yourself if you can work with everybody: even with your more 'difficult' colleagues. (It's easy to work with the accommodating people). Your colleagues are natural allies, and collaborating with allies increases your likelihood of success. Cooperate with and play to your colleagues' strengths to get the best performance out of them.

When it's obvious that you respect and acknowledge your colleagues, they are generally willing to work with you. Then there are times when they won't . . .

Colleagues will help you when:

1. You are very clearly and passionately working yourself, even if you are the project leader.

2. You have a demonstrated track record of success—everyone loves a winner!

3. You convince them that your project is important.

4. You are organized and make good use of everyone's time.

5. You acknowledge other's contributions—even if the contribution is limited to good counsel.

6. You share the rewards of success.

7. You buffer the team from major slings and arrows.

8. You model energetic and can-do behaviors, and have assembled a similar team with those characteristics.

9. You listen more than you talk.

10. You avoid asking your colleagues or team to do unnecessary or busy work (i.e., make charts!)

11. You are responsive to their requests for help.

12. You keep your word.

Colleagues will not help you when:

1. You appear uncertain yourself about the mission and cannot consistently represent yourself, your colleagues, or your the team well to management.

2. You cannot 'net' issues or drive issues to closure.

3. You are perceived as not being able to win.

4. Your task is perceived as unimportant.

5. Time is wasted, and issues are revisited and remain open for on-going discussion.

6. You talk more than you listen.

7. You cannot (or fail to) resolve team issues or roadblocks.

Your colleagues are your natural allies: you'll get the best contribution from others if you are trustworthy and collaborate.

8. You hoard credit and related rewards, and dole out blame.

9. You consistently model a lethargic or 'let's just try' vibe.

10. You don't 'own' the task at hand: you are merely asking your colleagues for help because "THEY" (the management team) want this task done.

11. You are too busy or self-important to respond to them when they need your help.

12. You don't keep your word.

When seeking help, you must examine your behavior and make sure that you are consistently exuding a high performance, committed, and positive vibe. Energy and a positive attitude attracts others, and attracting others is necessary when building a network. The more robust your network, the greater your odds are of getting help when you need it. Keep this in mind in all your interactions.

Attitude for altitude

If you are upbeat, gregarious, approachable, and think that you can do just about anything, chances are people love being around you. If you execute well, they also love working with you! Martin E.P. Seligman asserts in his book, *Learned Optimism,* "Research showed repeatedly that optimists do better in school, win more elections, and succeed more at work than pessimists do." No wonder we want to be around them. If the statement above does not describe you, perhaps a minor overhaul can help you draw others to you, while at the same time creating a better office environment for yourself and your peers. If you cannot be readily described as upbeat, approachable, and capable, please consider doing the following if you are not already:

1. Make eye contact and say hello—to everyone. When you are walking down corridors, get away from the walls and out into the middle of the hallway. Don't look at your shoes or off into space, or otherwise pretend to be lost in thought. Entering a conference room? Come to the front, don't hide in the back. There's no need to present yourself as timid. If we make ourselves small and unassuming, we make it hard for others to envision us leading projects and people. Can one really judge someone's leadership potential by how they walk down a hall or where they sit in a room? Absolutely not. But isn't it likely that others will make inferences about such a person moving vacantly down a hallway, hugging the wall, looking at his feet, or sitting in the back of a conference room perhaps peeping out a response to a greeting? What could one possibly be afraid of? Does such a person draw you to her? Is he or she someone you'd like to meet? How would you anyone know? Engage. Wear a smile on your face. Eye contact and smiles are good for the work climate/environment. Everyone wants to be around someone who is happy and upbeat. If you're shy, you're shy, but wear your game face to work.

2. If you are in the office, don't isolate yourself: leave the office door open unless you need to *temporarily* shut it for discretion or privacy, or because you really need to work without being disturbed. If a shut door is your norm, you are really signaling that you do not want to engage with your colleagues. Being approachable is the first step to building the work environment you want, and the network you'll need. Even if you are working remotely, make yourself available and accessible.

3. Act purposefully. Energy attracts. Don't stroll casually down the hall or meander to and from

the cafeteria at lunchtime. You're getting paid, aren't you? Don't you have somewhere to go, something to do? So get there. A leisurely pace is for the beach. There are some exceptions to this rule of thumb, and a REAL mentor will concede them: if you are lost in deep thought or working with someone as you walk, by all means, proceed at your own pace. If you are not doing those things, proceed at the company pace.

4. Limit complaints. If something is worth complaining about, please try to help fix it, or point it out to someone who is better prepared or has the capability to fix it. If you can't fix it, it's fine to have minor comments in the spirit of team comraderie, but don't dwell on an "unfixable" problem, and don't make complaining a habit. Know how to complain acceptably in the office. If you want to commiserate with someone who is complaining, a knowing wink, a smirk, a roll of the eyes, or even a few catch phrases to allow others to laugh at your situation will work. The point will be taken, the listener will smile, but no one will be drained. Best of all, no one will nickname you "Drainer/Complainer" and try to avoid you as you walk down the hallway.

5. After a setback, dust yourself off and get back on the field. Everyone has missteps or setbacks. What is key is that you do not sulk and do not accept a mantle of failure. The only time to quit is after you've won or completely and hopelessly lost your funding. If you stumble, coach yourself back to the front line. Do not allow yourself more than a weekend to sulk or obsess over stumbles. Don't prolong self-doubt. Instead, be purposeful and keep going!

6. Be a person of action. As was discussed earlier, please never say that you are waiting for something from one of your colleagues, before you can complete whatever it is you have to do. Prefer to say that you need "x" from Bob, and list the things that **you** are doing to get them from Bob. In this way, you continue to make progress where you need to do so. Don't waste time, and don't be willing to wait.

Leaders can't have their 'toe on the line'.
—*Janette Bombardier*

---

7. Avoid making disparaging comments about your peers and managers. Please note that you always take a personal risk when you make disparaging comments about others. None of us really knows all of the alliances of our colleagues, and some alliances shift over time. It is best to avoid commentary altogether, though, if pressed to contribute something to a 'gripe session', you can always offer up something neutral (i.e., "No matter what, I am just going to keep going.") You need not martyr yourself, you just don't want to get caught up in needless risk-taking behavior.

8. Don't make anyone question your comportment. Ideally, we are all cooperative and collaborative at work. With regard to your comportment, you want to be considered a solid citizen, with no hint of "difficult to work with", "is disrespectful", or "doesn't get along with men or women", etc. Additionally, your integrity should be above reproach. There's no 'testing the limits' on this front. If you want to be successful, in all your interactions, your "toe" should be nowhere near crossing the line.

9. Ask others how they are, and inquire about their business at work. Have an 'elevator speech' ready to go. This one-to—two minute summary captures the highlights of what you and your team are doing. If things aren't going well, smile and tell the person inquiring to ask in a month—then ask about his/her business. The elevator speech isn't always about great news, and it isn't always about perfection, but it is always always about selling, and it's always net, positive and upbeat.

10. Avoid negative people and vampires. They will drain you, period.

11. Don't take it personally, it's only business.

12. Listen to other people talk about their work. This is a martial arts maxim: "Don't let your cup get too full." You can never know enough, and "engineering curiosity" helps everyone learn more.

13. Always offer to help, then follow-through.

The elevator speech isn't always about perfection, but it is always about selling: it's net and positive.

Mentoring Maxim

Real Mentors Tell You:
Don't Be the Office Leak.

Every office has a "leak." Everyone in the office knows who the "leak" is, except for maybe the leak. The "leak" is usually 'coin-operated,' meaning that you can offer her a small bit of information, and in exchange, she will spill her guts on the latest gossip and around-the-coffee-machine rumors. Nobody wants to tell the leak that she is a leak, because after all, the leak is an excellent and even entertaining source of news. On the other hand, most people understand that they cannot share meaningful information, or information that must be kept quiet, with the leak. The leak cannot be trusted, and a lack of trust in the office directly translates into a lack of success. It's fun and satisfying to be the person "in the know," but since trust is such a valuable commodity, 'close to the vest' will serve you more than 'get it off your chest.'

Real mentors tell you: while you can profit from his information, don't you become the office leak.

How to REALLY build your networks

So you've convinced yourself that you already execute well, know how to net, inspect, collaborate, walk and talk like a leader, and engage with your colleagues. However, despite these qualities, you are still perplexed by the perpetual office problem: how do you get the world to realize that you are both essential and the next great leader that the world is waiting for? You will have to take the usual steps that your organization stipulates or does as a matter of protocol (i.e., fill out whatever forms are necessary so that you can formally contend for any competitive job opening management reviews). These are things that are necessary and good, however but remain largely outside of your control. They are not, however, the only options open to you. Below are a few tried and true ideas for meeting people (and potential mentors) that are entirely within your control:

1. Remember the recommendation to make eye contact and engage? Well now you're going to need it—so I trust you're doing it with everyone you encounter, especially those folks you see on a routine basis.

2. Introduce yourself after you've been making eye contact and saying hello for some period of time. Simply say, "Hi, I'm Pat. I've seen you in the hallway now for a couple of weeks and while we always say hello, we've never been formally introduced." Do not end this brief contact until you know what area this new person works in and what they do there. They will likely ask the same of you. Be sure to greet them by name the next you meet them, and do have some small exchange, upon which you can build.

3. You can 'target' people that you'd like to meet, and have the same interaction. All you need is a

hallway or a coffee machine. If you are around when your 'contact' is around, you can take the initiative to introduce yourself. I am not suggesting that you "stalk" anyone, but most people have routines—regular schedules that you can leverage just for that quick exchange that can later lead to something more profound. None of these early exchanges should take longer than a couple of minutes. If the 'coffee bar' closes every morning at 10:00 for example, and you know that there will be a mad rush to get there before 10:00, then between 9:45-10:05 is likely a good time to encounter people you want to meet.

4. If a new person you've met works in an area that interests you, or has a skill that you'd like to tap, during one of your exchanges ask him or her if you can tell them quickly about something that you are working on. Perhaps you can do that while walking with them to their next a meeting or the cafeteria for coffee, etc. Tell them what you are doing and ask them what they think about it. If there's no time, ask if you can schedule fifteen minutes (*not more!*) on their calendar to discuss it.

> *The Fifteen Minute Rule: ask and prepare for 15 minutes of review and interview.*

5. When that time arrives, stick to the fifteen minutes. Don't leave without asking two final questions: a) can you come back again in a month or so again for fifteen minutes to review the project again and b) is there an expert on their team whom they would recommend that you meet? In this way, once you follow-up that lead, you'll have added yet another expert to your network, and you have the opportunity to keep working with the new person you wanted to meet in the first place. Most importantly, because you are demonstrating what you are *doing* in your current project, you are effectively *interviewing* with the person you are meeting

101

with. Don't be casual about these fifteen minute sessions: prepare.

6. Can't bump into someone you'd like to meet in the hallway? Call their office anyway and tell them that you are working on "Project of the Future" and would like to get fifteen minutes on their calendar to tell them what you are doing and to get their thoughts on your plan. Almost everyone will clear fifteen minutes for you—*if you have a plan to review*. If you have no plan or ideas, it will be difficult to get a high performance leader to make time to meet you. Always honor the fifteen minutes you requested.

7. If you are leading a project, you can establish a board of directors for your project. Tap experts from multiple areas and tell them that you'd like them to act as consultants for the project. Explain that they will be invited to exactly one meeting per month or per quarter, for one hour, in which they will listen to the project status and then will be asked to provide their thoughts. Assure them that they will not otherwise pick up action items or assignments to complete. They are simply going to be a 'brain trust' that you tap—and coincidently, one that will get to see you in action—leading and executing.

8. You can also, independent of a project, contact people you'd like to meet simply because they've had experiences or successes you'd like to learn about or emulate. Most people will clear a half hour on their calendars for this. Over time, you can always ask to come back and show them your plan to achieve the same. Always have something to show this potential new mentor.

9. Initiate a project. Start something—a support group, an educational group, or pick something that needs attention but has no real owner managing it—and step up to lead the effort. Recruit others to help. Invite interested parties to a "results" session. You will have the opportunity to meet new people doing this, while developing and displaying leadership skills.

10. Take a job in a new area—even if it's only a temporary assignment. Make it a point to meet and spend some time with everyone.

11. Volunteer to help at a company-sponsored event that you would not otherwise be invited to, especially if it's being held locally. This may cost you a vacation day or two, but that expense may be outweighed by, for example, meeting all of the senior sales or engineering teams at regional sales or training conferences because you worked the registration desk. If you opt to volunteer, look for opportunities to work with participants at the start of an event. Towards the end of an event, attendee thoughts tend to turn toward home.

12. Take a Technical Assistant's (TA) job when you are at middle management level, but don't know the organization's leadership team very well. TA's perform a lot of grunt work as they assist executives or senior leaders in the management of the more mundane components of the leader's business unit. The TA manages the executive schedule, researches and develops presentations, speeches or other collateral that the executive needs. He prepares assignments or follow-ups in response to requests from the executive's own management chain or peer group. The TA makes sure that the executive's team is aware of and working on any commitment the executive has made or needs to or intends to

make. She will host visitors, plan travel, and handle all day to day administrative matters. In general, under the guidance of the executive, the TA runs the executive office, freeing the executive to think, collaborate with peers and partners, and guide her team. Despite this workload, the TA spends the day shadowing her executive and can only begin to work once the executive's day has ended. In exchange for this often grueling schedule, because she shadows her executive, the TA is privy to the management of a business at senior executive levels. She has frequent access to her executive's network. *A wise TA then, will make sure she has an important, non-adminstrative assignment or project to deliver, in addition to performing her normal duties.* The TA assignment will have been of less service to the TA if the boss' network has observed only that the TA makes terrific slides for her boss. Remember, I have asked you to always have something to demonstrate when engaging a mentor or potential mentors. TA positions are competitive. They are tough to get, and tough to manage if you can get them, but to the extent that you can leverage your executive's network by demonstrating to the leadership team what you are capable of, you can dramatically increase your own growth opportunities.

In net, it's your task to meet as many people as you can, and to demonstrate to that audience how you think, how you comport yourself, and how much you can get accomplished. Note, in each case, you have been advised to show your contact what you are working on. You are not merely getting input, you are also taking the opportunity to show that you know how to develop a plan, articulate and sell it, and execute to it. Using this methodology, you can substantially grow your network by yourself, and significantly increase your potential for growth and recognition and relatedly, career growth.

Mentoring Maxim

Real Mentors Tell You:
Start Growing Your Network Early

Here is a true statement: the further you progress in your career, the more you will need to have successful leaders who will assert that they know and trust your work, as well as support your efforts to get promoted. If you are in a technical community, for example, advanced senior technical professionals may be called upon to agree that you have demonstrated a level of proficiency to warrant promotion to senior levels. If this is a given in your organization, you obviously have to know many of these people, and they have to know you and your work. You can wait (there's that word) until your paths cross, when and if they do, or you can create opportunities to meet them, get to know them, and show them your work well before you need their "stamp of approval." A real mentor tells you to create opportunities for yourself **now**.

Ask these leaders for an interview or shadow time. Draft them to be consultants for your projects, and don't hesitate to ask them to act as mentors. Engage, be proactive, and prepare to grow.

Regina Darmoni

Endnote:

Martin E.P. Seligman, *Learned Optimism*, New York, Free Press, 1998, page 97.

CHAPTER 8

Real Mentors Tell You:
Enlarge and Charge—Prepare for Your Next Job

Positioning yourself for progress

When you are a new hire in a firm, whether in your first professional assignment or joining a firm as an experienced professional, you will more than likely depend on your hiring manager to help you succeed in your new job and to help you find your "next" position in the company. The time of your "point of entry" job is the first and last time that you want to be entirely dependent upon your manager to help you navigate your career ladder. By analyzing your own level of competitiveness relative to your peers, by developing skills that will distinguish you from your peers, by growing your network, and by positioning yourself to take risks—*the right risks*—you can do quite a lot, independent of others, to propel yourself to the top.

Standing out in a competitive market

Any beginning business school student can wax poetic about SWOT (Strengths, Weaknesses, Opportunities, Threats) diagrams, and any marketer worth his salt can draw one up as part of an analysis of his ability to win against his competition. In order to progress, it's important to know your strengths and know which skills are lacking. A personalized SWOT diagram is an excellent tool for promoting a frank and on-going self-assessment, and its results should necessarily drive a personal commitment to improve your competitiveness relative to your peers. With results well understood, you should of your own volition, routinely investigate available opportunities that can augment your skills and minimize weaknesses.

We don't have to take the word "threat" here too literally. When doing your personal SWOT, you want to know either who specifically or what kinds of candidates are competing with you for a promotion or any other recognition you desire, and using that information, you need to start working to develop a competitive edge. For example, if you are a candidate for a business line "profit and loss" leadership job, and other candidates are more competitive because they have accounting skills that you lack, you may need to enroll in some specialized accounting classes or take a preparatory assignment that will give you more solid financial skills. In a world where the most competitive person wins, you must proactively assure that you are that person.

Another way to stand out from the competition is to have "distinguishing" growth experiences. You want to look for a position that will give you skills that you could not readily acquire by continuing to work solely in your area of expertise. If you are not free to change jobs, or are uninterested in leaving your current organization, you can seek a "stretch" assignment whereby you temporarily take on a challenge role. Such an assignment would typically require you to demonstrate some sort of proficiency that you have not yet had the opportunity to display, or perhaps you would be given the opportunity to display that proficiency on a larger scale. You would be expected to perform the extra assignment in addition to your normal duties.

Marketing your strengths is as important as building and demonstrating them. Not only is it important

Ensure that several members of your leadership team—not just your immediate manager—are aware of your contributions.

that you are aware of your strengths, it is also vitally important that your leadership team is aware of them. You should *ensure* that several members of the leadership team—not just your manager—are aware of your contributions. It is obviously better if they can see you in action, rather than having to be subjected to a personal "commercial" from you. Your effective marketing—perhaps through that network that you've worked to establish—will also help you at reward time.

When deciding who has been a standout, and deserves special recognition and/or reward consideration, the leadership team—and let's be perfectly clear, during times of scarce resources in a large organization, a **team** is going to have input—will review all of the high-performance candidates. The last thing you want, dear reader, is for your manager to bring up your name and have other managers or leaders respond, "*Who?*"

While it would be preferable that our managers and peers be innately aware of our successes (and blind to our missteps), we may have to help them remember what we've contributed over the course of any evaluation period. It is in our best interests to do this elegantly. Before you sound your horn, you have to ask yourself, honestly if you have made a substantive contribution to an important project, or if you have merely "touched" it (meaning you've worked on it briefly, or merely provided some input). If it's the latter, store up this good will for later.

If you have made a significant contribution, ideally you'll be recognized anyway, but you should consider sending a brief memo to the project leader and his/her manager stating that consistent with your commitment, you have completed your deliverables for Project Awesome and are now officially leaving the project and starting to work on Project Amazing. Invite the project leader and his/her manager to call you if they have questions or require additional actions from you. You will invariably get a response acknowledging your contributions and thanking you for your efforts. These memos are very useful for summarizing results throughout the year. *Systematically* submitting them in summary form to your management teams for their use in evaluating your team and individual contributions is also a good idea. For example, if you are a team leader, you can send a *brief, quarterly* team status memo to your teammates and your respective managers indicating what you and your team or colleagues have accomplished so far, and what that means to the business. I.e., "At the end of the third quarter, Team Outstanding has completed 90% of its annual goals, ahead of plan pace, leading to $10M of improvements (20% above plan) in manufacturing throughput." Make it easy for your manager and other leaders to recognize your contributions and reward you while at the same time making it easy for other leaders to consider hiring you for growth assignments. To get the next job you want, execute well and make sure the leadership **team** is aware of your work.

Right move, wrong time

How to choose your "next" position is a great discussion topic for you and your mentors. In weighing the criteria for taking a new job, especially when a promotion or leadership opportunity is involved, you want to be especially thoughtful about making the right move at the wrong time. Some "growth" opportunities may be presented to you too soon for you to fully take advantage of all of their expected benefits. While these opportunities would never be *wasted*, they would not be fully *leveraged*, and this is to be avoided.

As an example, let's revisit the TA position that was discussed in an earlier chapter. Recall that in

> *Don't take the 'right' job too early.*

exchange for the grueling schedule and not-so-glamorous assignments, the TA gets access to the executive's network. After demonstrating her ability to execute, lead, net, collaborate, etc, the successful TA can reasonably expect some type of leadership assignment at the end of the TA assignment. If the successful TA is already a senior level employee, she can either leverage the TA assignment into a promotional opportunity, or into a leadership assignment that will position her to compete for a promotion in the near future.

Suppose, however, that an employee is offered a TA position earlier—before becoming a "senior" level employee. That same employee, under the same successful conditions, will then complete the TA assignment and find himself positioned to become a "senior" level employee. Alternately, he may be offered an assignment that will position him to compete for a promotion to "senior" level. If this employee could have become a "senior" level employee without having taken the TA position, then he would not have fully leveraged the benefits the TA job offered. In that case, he should have taken the TA job later in his career when he was more senior. Why? If he was already a senior level employee, the executive network he would gain access to would be more willing to put him in, or position him for, a leadership role following successful completion of his TA assignment.

Build a bench: training your replacement enables you to take new assignments more readily.

You must always think about how far up the ladder you can go when following the 'traditional' career path in your organization. Your goal is to look for growth opportunities to propel you farther than you would get otherwise. Unless the "guiding hands" of your mentors direct you differently given your personal situation, in general, you should not waste growth assignments getting to levels that you believe you can achieve as a matter of course.

That first management job

Before you can run a division, lead the foreign bureau, have a seat on the board of directors, or become the CEO, you must get your first management job. This initial foray into management should meet the following minimum criteria:

- Have deliverables that are readily measurable and that are important to the organization. This is essential in order for you to demonstrate and claim success. Working on critical projects is the best way to ensure that your accomplishments are 'visible'.

- Offer some degree of visibility beyond your immediate management chain (meaning that other leaders are aware of your objectives, progress and final results).

- Offer the opportunity to lead a reasonable number of employees (with reasonable being defined per the norms of your organization).

- Offer "stretch" assignment opportunities, meaning that you can branch out to do more than you've been asked to do, even if you have to create these opportunities yourself.

The management assignment is your opportunity to demonstrate that in addition to managing the departmental workload, you can also lead people in a manner that harnesses their skills, ensuring that they are working toward the good of the organization as well as enabling them to build their own careers. Besides your ability to execute or deliver, as a manager, you will be assessed on your judgment, discretion, character, integrity and leadership. The first management assignment is typically the gateway to the top of the organization, so the sooner you get this management "stripe" and perform successfully, the sooner you can find yourself on the way to the top.

Minimizing debt to maximize your flexibility

We all understand that flexibility is essential to maximizing our growth potential. We need to and want to be poised to take any good and timely growth assignments that come our way. One way to prepare oneself for that possibility is to train a replacement—someone who will only need to come up a minor learning curve to step effectively into your role.

Another way to do it is to maintain a personal debt-light financial position. Someone mired in debt may be ill-prepared to take career risks. Instead of managing his career, he finds himself managed—*by his debt*. Investment debt is a good thing, but debt for personal consumption has to be avoided. What if you want to quit your job? What if you want to try an assignment that is such a stretch for you and your organization that you risk utter failure, but are promised great rewards if you perform well? What if you want to supplement your skills by volunteering for a once-in-a-lifetime—but unpaid—internship? What if you want to go back to school? Too much debt may preclude you from taking advantage of any of those scenarios. Not only is it liberating to rid yourself of debt, eliminating debt will also enable you to grow your bank balance and potentially, with more risk-tolerance, your career opportunities. While you are staying out of debt, it is also a good idea to carefully look after the funds you amass. Many people are casual about the management of their investment portfolio, believing that as long as they leave their investments alone (relatively speaking) over the long run, they'll be okay. That may prove to be true, but acknowledging that robust finances allow for more life options or more flexibility, paying attention to your growing funds is warranted.

If you're a new professional hire, you've probably been living off a limited budget and now you are earning a full-time professional salary. You take your first apartment (college housing doesn't count) and after that, what is your first priority? For most of us, it's a vehicle. Others think they absolutely need a new stereo. And no matter how casual the office atmosphere, you'll probably need a wardrobe upgrade. All of these items, even the new stereo, are understandable. What is not so understandable is going on a buying spree to furnish that new apartment, especially if the spree is funded by credit card debt. And that vehicle? Does it have to be a BMW? (Not that there's anything wrong with a BMW—quite the contrary!) While of course you'll look fabulous behind the wheel of a luxury car, you may find that its purchase locks you into a financial situation that stresses you and plays havoc with your budget.

What if you discover that you don't like your job? Or the company? What if you love the company but not the location, and you can't get a transfer? Staying out of debt is the key to flexibility, and flexibility is key to making good career decisions. You don't want to keep a job because you "have to," and your company will not likely want that either. Also, you don't want to avoid risky career moves because you've mired yourself in debt and now feel that you have to limit yourself to safe career choices. In the first few years of working full time, concentrate on eliminating the necessary debt you have created (that car note, school loans, etc.) and saving as much of your salary as you can.

Aside from what has been stated above, the best counsel I can provide is to tell you that if you are committed to avoiding debt or getting out of debt, please avail yourself of books written by any of the top money counselors of our day: Suzy Orman, Rick Edelman, Jim Cramer, Jane Bryant Quinn, to name a few. You know the basics. You know to maximize your contribution to your company 401K plan. You're also building up a six month rainy day fund. Terrific. So what's to discuss here? Just the fact that many people have a hands-off approach to money management: in fact, they don't "manage" at all, but benignly neglect.

I went to a retirement party for an executive who, during his farewell speech, took time out from saying goodbye to his colleagues to urge mid-life and new employees to manage their money. He was on his way to a very comfortable retirement and forewarned us that if we wanted the same in the near future, we should make time at least once a week to sit down and work on improving our financial position. This retiring executive reminded us that we were entering our peak earning years and now was the time to take advantage of that by maximizing and managing our savings. He urged us not to be too busy *today* to ensure a comfortable *tomorrow*. I pass this excellent advice on to you.

Managing your money helps you to maximize your flexibility.

Mentoring Maxim

Real Mentors Tell You:
Find Distinguishing Experiences

As you grow in your career, particularly if you are not a generalist but have specialized (i.e., you are an accountant or circuit designer or web designer, etc), you can potentially to win more promotional opportunities over the competition if you have unique experiences that other specialists in your area have not had. Look for opportunities where you can make use of some of your existing strengths while at the same time developing some new skills.

• In Marketing? Try a stint in Sales.

• In Finance? Take an assignment in Operations.

• In Manufacturing? Try a Supply Chain leadership position.

• In Research? Take a role in Manufacturing.

Use the transference of skills—especially if you plan to go back to your old area—to create something new or to improve existing systems. Getting your ticket punched in a new area will enhance the "S" quadrant in your personal SWOT diagram and increase your opportunities for growth.

And, it goes without saying now, you'll grow your network as well.

PART II

QUESTIONS ASKED

CHAPTER 9

Mentoring Mojo

I have developed a mentoring and networking program called 'Mentoring Mojo' for various employee "constituencies" in my office. In addition to exploring the basic blocking and tackling techniques that are essential for success in the corporate world, the Mojo teams explore career growth inhibitors and improvement paths in an atmosphere that is open and conducive to group problem solving and exploration of sensitive topics in a secure forum. Following are select topics and questions that have come up in those Mojo sessions, or in conversations with mentees and mentors over the years . . .

—RMTYT—

Deciding on one job over another

If you are doing what I have already discussed earlier in this book, you are likely going to have a wealth of opportunities in your future. How to choose among them? A smart person once told me that when one door opens, others close behind you. That's not quite the same as "when one door closes, another opens." What my colleague meant was that each time you accept a new opportunity, you leave behind one (or many) potential careers, and set yourself on a path toward a more specialized career. If there's any truth to that notion, it means that when you take a new job, it must be one that creates a number of potential opportunities to compensate for the ones that will have gotten away by virtue of your having chosen the current one. None of this is to say that you can't go back and re-open a door that you once closed, but doors do close.

With that in mind, make certain that any position that you take adds something to your personal "tool box." A new job must bring with it the acquisition of new skills, and must increase your exposure to higher-level management and/or many more managers or leaders. To the tasks at hand, you will want to be able to bring to bear your existing skills, while at the same time integrating your newly acquired skill set, such that that the new whole becomes greater than the sum of the parts. Focus on developing skills that will be of use to you and your employer in your current position, as well as in the marketplace outside your firm. If you optimize to increase your own competitiveness, chances are you'll be optimizing for your firm as well. Though I cannot assert that it is true, Jack Welch, former CEO of General Electric, was said to have told his employees at GE that he was "glad to have them ready to go, happy to have them stay." He knew that if they were skilled enough to be able to leave at a moment's notice, it was good for GE to have them stay.

> *Consider new jobs if they offer the opportunity to learn competitive and transferable skills.*

Some Do's and Don'ts to consider when weighing a new job decision:

- Do not take a lateral move that does little more for you than get you out of a job that you've out-grown, or that simply liberates you from any current dissatisfaction.

- Don't take a promotion simply because it's a promotion and/or because there's more money associated with it. Do take it if there is more growth opportunity, offers more visibility to significant leaders, and permits you to both learn and demonstrate new skills.

- Don't take a job merely because the current manager is charismatic. People change jobs all the time. If the charismatic manager has something to teach you, ask if he or she will mentor you.

- Do consider that customer-facing jobs (those positions in which you interact directly with the firm's clients), when performed successfully, confer very useful, portable, and competitive skills. Working directly with clients means you are working directly with the firm's life-blood. In today's economy, you owe it to yourself to be as competitive as possible, at all times. Make sure you have at least a rotational assignment in a client-facing position.

- Don't take a job if your temperament and managerial style clash wildly with that of your new leadership team. If yours is a laid-back persona, more accustomed to dealing with long-range planning, whereas the new office is hurried and aggressive and primarily focused on near-end results, chances are this is a marriage that will not be successful—unless you are the partner who is willing to change.

- What is the maturity level of the project or initiative: is it in "start-up" mode or are you joining a mature team? Do consider whether you are a fit for the "A" team or the "B" team. The "A" team is the group that is convened at the start of a new endeavor. They have a mission, a badge, and a blank canvas. The "B" team is the team that takes over after either the "A" team has successfully made a go of an initiative, or if they have failed at it. Some people are comfortable being part of or leading a visionary and risk-tolerant "A"

> *If you are risk-adverse, think hard before taking an "A-team" job.*

team. Others prefer the existing infrastructure and somewhat lesser risk of "B" teams.

Take your time, choose wisely—for yourself and your company.

Evaluating job offers from former colleagues/friends and family

Suppose you are fortunate enough to get a call from a former colleague who has moved on to a new firm. He or she is happy in the new position and thinks you will be perfect for an opening they have in the marketing department. How do you decide if you should go or not? This is actually an easy question to answer.

- First, before you throw away all of the personal brand equity you have built up with your current firm, you must ask yourself if you have honestly exhausted all possibility of making the progress there that you desire. If you haven't, you owe it to yourself to work on that angle first.

- Second, were you contemplating leaving, or did you start thinking about leaving when the "bluebird" offer flew into your window? If you weren't thinking about moving prior to the job offer, chances are you really aren't that dissatisfied, and again, you owe it to yourself to pursue internal opportunities for advancement before jumping ship. Brand equity is a valuable thing, and you'll have to build it up again wherever you wind up working.

- Third, you must dispassionately assess where your friend or family member is placed in the new company. If you are thinking about going to join someone who is a lower level manager, the danger is that you will be taking on a lot of risk for whatever gains you will have made, even if you follow the above evaluation recommendations. You are still contemplating leaving behind a network of people who already know you. Assuming that whatever renown you have at your current firm is positive, that "name recognition" factor has some value. You must weigh if it's worth it to give that up to cast your lot with someone who is himself still a relative "unknown" in the hierarchy of the new firm.

Some folks will be comfortable with these odds. I personally would not leave an established position in a high-performance organization to join another firm under the tutelage or guidance of someone who is not even in middle management. We all need some mentoring, even if it only happens at the beginning of a career or when entering a new position. We want—and are best served—by getting that mentoring from someone who has already demonstrated that she knows how to be successful in the new organization. I don't like even odds. *Before leaving your company, make sure that the person you are going to join has a demonstrated track record.*

When you're in trouble

It's uncomfortable to be in trouble. Trouble is wide-ranging: it can include being temporarily being in the "red" on a project, receiving a disappointing annual performance appraisal, performing poorly on a key audit, or making a faux pas in the wrong meeting with the wrong person or client. Trouble can also mean that you've done something overtly or intentionally wrong. Each of these cases drives different remedies, but two things are a constant: 1) you want to get out of trouble ASAP and 2) how you behave when you are in trouble can be a huge factor in how long you remain in trouble. Obviously, your objective is to get out of trouble quickly.

> *How you behave when you're in trouble will be a factor in how quickly you get out of trouble.*

Let's look at ways to address various kinds of trouble:

"The project is under-performing" trouble

If you've allowed a project status to turn "red," you already know from the chapter on execution what you need to do to right your ship. You'll need to project a new and realistic time line to recover (albeit aggressive, because after all, you are under-performing), assign action owners, get help, and manage people and actions to guarantee that that you will meet your revised timeline. While you are recovering to the plan, you should always project your most elegant, professional persona, no matter how much of a "squeeze" management exerts. Don't make excuses and don't blame others. You are going to sweat, and I think it's okay to let "them" see you sweat. Don't take off anyone's head in response to the pressure: you've "earned" that pressure by under-performing. Please behave elegantly while fixing your problems.

"Disappointing performance evaluation" trouble

Note that I didn't say "bad," I said "disappointing." It is predictable that following a disappointing performance review, an employee will return to her office, shut the door, and call someone significant in her life with whom she can share the news. That's the right thing to do. The wrong thing to do is to allow that news to "leak" into your behavior in the office. Receiving a disappointing performance appraisal should be a catalyst to make you honestly re-evaluate your annual performance and define a new path that will get you to the performance level and relatedly, to the appraisal level you desire. This path must include regular interlocks with your manager to assure that you both agree on what needs to be done, as opposed to what is currently being done, to get you on your desired path. It's hard to hide your disappointment, but a disappointing appraisal does not give you license to channel your inner Rasputin. This is not a time to avoid or ignore your manager. Do not stop communicating with your manager; do not treat the manager rudely; and do not attempt to subvert him in any way. On the contrary, you want to spend more time with your manager to make sure you are seeing eye to eye. At least once a quarter, if not more frequently, please discuss how you are doing, what the management team expects of you versus what you are actually delivering, and how you can improve matters if necessary. You need information, and this is the only way to get it. Do not wait (There's that admonishment again!) until the end of the year or the first half of the year to find out that the boss doesn't think you are doing well. Such a delay will cost you money in missed rewards and delays in achieving the success you desire. Talk early, talk often.

Privately, take some time, but not a lot of time, to sulk if you need to, but then you must re-focus your energy on improvement. To get your head back into the game, focus on nailing the next key events per the plan, and if there aren't any, create some. Find something meaningful to contribute to the team. You want to "ante up" as soon as possible and you need to demonstrate to yourself that despite the disappointing performance evaluation, you can get back to execution, execution, execution—and relatedly, to success. To the extent that you can professionally manage your "persona" during this period, you'll be considered a class act.

"I've done something really wrong" trouble

If you've done something terribly wrong, but you're still working for your company, the good news is that you are not fired. The bad news is that you're in the penalty box. From the penalty box, you will want to behave exactly as you would if you had a project that was late—with two exceptions: 1) realize you have amends to make and a reputation to recover, and 2) the penalty box is no place to call attention to yourself. The penalty box is all about quiet, consistent execution. The way to get out of the penalty box is to consistently deliver everything asked of you—and more—while flying beneath the radar. No whining is required or tolerable.

Trouble and your extra-curricular activities

I've already suggested to you that one way to demonstrate leadership, grow your network, and learn some new skills is to get involved and even start a new and compelling initiative of some sort. Volunteerism and self-initiative can be a terrific boon to your career—except when they become a distraction, or are perceived as distractions by your leadership team. While doing a self-assessment for your annual performance review you find that you list under "accomplishments" either more, or an equal number of volunteer or 'extra curricular' events as your work-related assignments, it is likely that your not-directly-work-related volunteerism is a distraction. This applies even to quasi-work related volunteerism like chairing industry committees or writing for technical publications in your field. You can assume that your management team will do the mental math as well, especially if your performance is not exceptional or if your management team is somewhat undecided about your level of performance. Though well-intentioned, too much volunteerism or extra-curricular activity can be detrimental to career growth. Your commitment to execution means putting the primary responsibilities of your day job first.

Signs of trouble—the physical things:

We've already established that it's okay to let our leaders see you sweat. Here are a few martial artist tools to help you avoid showing them some things you don't want them to see:

Tears

Hold your head up straight. With your head fixed in this upright position, look up with intense concentration. Don't move your head while looking up like that. This simple move will block your lacrimal ducts and prevent you from crying.

Nervousness/Shaking

You must control your breathing to keep your nerves at bay. When not under stress, practice slowing down your breathing. Inhale, using as much time as you can to take that one breath. Exhale the same way. You should not focus on expanding your lung and chest area, but rather on expanding your belly. Expand the abdomen as you practice this slow breathing exercise and take note of your slower heart rate. Under this level of breathing discipline, the body resists a racing heart or pulse rate, both of which contribute to feeling nervous and shaking. If you are anticipating a problematic situation, practice this breathing pre-emptively so that when your big moment comes, your body is calmed.

If you already 'in the spotlight' and find yourself obviously nervous, slow down your pace. Give yourself breathing room.

Gulping

Continued gulping is another sign of nervousness and may indicate shallow breathing. Chances are you are talking too fast and too long for the volume of air that you have in your lungs. Stop talking and take a slow, deep breath before you resume. Hum

Hold it together: breathe and block your lacrimal ducts.

(say 'hmm') or laugh if you have the opportunity to do so unobtrusively. Speak slower and in shorter sentences until you have your breathing under control.

Needing feedback versus being needy

We all need feedback in order to do our jobs well, and feedback will likely be forthcoming even if we don't desire it. No one is exempt. Even the CEO of a Fortune 100 firm will get feedback from his Board of Directors and his shareholders. Feedback can be a catalyst for improvement or confirmation that we are correctly proceeding apace. However, there is a point wherein an employee seeks out too much feedback. You know that you have crossed over from needing feedback to being needy if:

- You must have feedback now—right now!—without necessarily being mindful of your manager's or colleagues' business demands.

- Your manager or colleagues must meet with you—per your request and noticeably more often than they do with your peers—in order to assure you that you are on track.

- You cannot enjoy or "allow" a colleague to be in the spotlight without having to interject something about your project or team.

- You spend more time asking your manager what the organization can do for you, rather than telling her what you have done for the organization.

In pursuit of feedback, and in avoidance of being perceived as needy, there are some times to avoid requesting feedback of any sort:

- The last few weeks of any quarter, when the organization is fully focused on, and in the home stretch of achieving its quarterly goals.

- When your manager or colleague is having a particularly bad time himself—maybe having just flubbed a client meeting, or received some bad news in his personal life.

- When your manager or colleague is preparing for an imminent big event, key deliverable, or client meeting.

- When your manager or colleague is preparing to leave for vacation later that day, or has just returned from vacation.

- First thing in the morning, as your manager or colleague is walking in the door.

- When your manager or colleague is engaged in a work-related conversation about something else.

If you are perceived as being needy, you are not perceived as a leader.

On being connected

Working remotely

This is a terrific idea for the organization as well as for the employee, as long as the employee does not completely disappear. In order to thrive, employees need a network, and they cannot effectively build that network from the comfort of their home office. Even if you need to spend most of your time at home, make sure you show up in the office once a week or so. Come to key team meetings and all recognition events. If you are not building a network, you are risk-tolerant and

> *Working remotely doesn't mean disappearing completely. Make it a priority to get back to base from time to time.*

you are completely dependent upon your manager to look after your career interests. Real Mentors tell you, quite simply: get to the office.

Your manager works remotely

This can be a real challenge for an employee. You must do your best to stay connected to your manager without overwhelming her with phone calls and emails. The best course of action is to set up a regular review schedule with your manager, with the intention of furthering your relationship and reviewing your projects. Nothing can replace face time, so even if the two of you are not in the same location, there must be occasions at least once or twice a year when you can meet and actually sit down together. In the meantime, you must make good use of your phone time together. You must be "net" about what you've accomplished to date, what your next steps will be, and the help you need. Always focus your conversations on the incremental progress you have made since your last review. Because we are now a telecommuter society, "out of sight" is not exactly "out of mind," but you can help your manager by emphasizing the results you're producing. Also note that maze bright employee will still make it a point to "see" his manager as often as possible under these circumstances.

<u>On mentors</u>

The mentor I've been assigned is a senior level person. I feel like I'm bothering him when I schedule time with him. How often should I see him and what should I ask?

How often you and your mentor meet very much depends on your needs and your respective schedules. Sometimes once a quarter is appropriate, sometimes once a year. It's appropriate to have all of the usual "next moves" and "what if" talks with your mentor, but I'd also encourage you to explore some of the topics in this book together. Don't worry about your mentor's "busyness." Most people want to help, and if you make good, prepared use of your time together, you'll always be able to get time on their calendars. Also note that it infrequently happens that one meeting is enough.

No matter how often you arrange to see your mentor, please be flexible about having to move the meetings due to last minute schedule changes. Don't take a rescheduled meeting personally, just understand that the needs of the business dictate it. I've heard employees say that they feel that managers and mentors indicate that they don't care about these sessions if they reschedule too many times. Mentors and managers are sensitive to this concern. Please point out a tendency to reschedule, if that seems to be happening a lot. Perhaps the two of you can agree on a better, less hectic day or hour to meet.

I am not trying to become President of the company. I like my position and work-life balance just the way it is. Do I still need a mentor?

This is a terrific scenario, but yes, you can still benefit from having mentors. Just because you are currently happy doesn't mean that you will always be, or that things around you won't change. You still need to work on building your network for tomorrow. Remember, you are risk-tolerant if you are only looking to your current manager to help you find career opportunities. Please limit your risk.

I either don't feel comfortable with my assigned mentor, or I just don't think there's anything more to gain from her. How do I end this relationship with no hard feelings (or without hurting my career)?

Not to worry. There is a natural end to a mentoring relationship, and you will both know it when you get there. Even if you get along well with your mentor and have found your time together useful, you can still lessen the frequency of your meetings, and quickly move to meeting on an "as needed" basis. Everyone is busy, and, generally speaking, while we are all happy to help, we are happy to conclude as well.

On new assignments

I don't know what I can do next because I don't know what's out there. How can I find out what kinds of jobs are really out there?

This is where building your network really pays off. This concern can be more easily managed than most employees think. You don't need a formal system of "jobs available" to help you, though you should certainly avail yourself of such a list if one exists. With this list, look at jobs that are suitable for your current level and skill set, as well as those that demand more. Pay attention to the descriptions (and the verbs!) of the higher level jobs so that you know where you need to aim as you complete your personal SWOT. In addition to this, talk to people about what they do. Go to general/open presentations; attend analyst briefings and quarterly reviews; talk to people as you walk together in the hallway, and ask them to give you fifteen minutes on their calendars. Ask if you can "shadow" senior leaders from various organizations for a day or two. Volunteer to do something charitable for the organization, then take the opportunity to meet people and learn. Get out there and network, and make it a priority to learn who is doing what.

What's a reasonable time frame for expecting to get an overseas assignment? What's a reasonable time frame for expecting to get my first

> *Job descriptions, especially for higher level positions, help you refine your competitive 'aim'.*

management job? What's a reasonable time frame for expecting my first executive assignment?

The answers to all three of these questions obviously depends on your organization's 'norms'. You don't have to accept "time served" as a rationale for growth or movement, but you can certainly use this as a yardstick. If you are in the corporate world, don't limit your yardstick to your department or even your function (i.e., accounting). Look to what happens in your division, other divisions, and your industry as well. If you know enough people, you can get good insight on this—which of course leads us back to the need to network. A management position and a foreign assignment all come after demonstration of good judgment as well as execution. Trust is a necessary selection criteria—as in *the leadership team must be able to trust you*—when it comes to other people's careers. And they will absolutely look for someone who will uphold acceptable behavior standards away from the unseeing eyes of the home office, etc. In any case, the answer to any of these questions should be, "When you are qualified and the most competitive fit for the job!" We all want to win that way.

On promotions

Why did they promote Bob over me?

They did not promote Bob over you. They simply promoted Bob. If you were doing your SWOT, Bob, or someone with Bob's skills, would have been on your radar. If Bob is from outside your division, or for some reason is unknown to you, simply ask your management team about the skill set that got Bob the promotion. If you ask correctly, I am confident that you will hear what unique skills Bob brought to the table. It is unlikely that you will hear that the reason Bob got the job was because Bob is the boss' nephew. Then once you know, get to work on your improvement plan. If you still think that you should have been promoted instead, again, please discuss this with your management team. You will have missed this opportunity, but if you handle the situation well, you can make sure that you are on the radar for the next opportunity.

Why did Bob get his recent promotion faster than I got mine?

Please refer to your SWOT and your corrective action plan. You can discuss with your management team why your promotion was not on your target schedule, what actions you need to take in order to be better positioned for promotion the next time, and how you can move up faster. My advice is to take a lot of responsibility and ownership here, and in your conversations with your leadership team, please do NOT talk about Bob. Talk about you.

On staying motivated

I want to quit

If you are an experienced employee, of course you have to decide if you are merely frustrated and having a challenging day (or week or month), or if you really have had it. Before you do anything rash, take a deep breath and call it a day. In fact, quit. For a day. Just quit. Pack up your briefcase or lunch box or extra shoes, shut down your machine, turn off the lights and leave-for the day. See how you feel 24 hours later. Sometimes that will be sufficient, knowing that it's in your power to leave it all behind if you want. If 48-72 hours later, you still feel the same way, then perhaps it is time for you to make a change. Conventional wisdom is that you want to have a new position lined up before you leave. I would amend conventional wisdom to say something *better* lined up. If you do leave, leave gracefully. As long as you leave elegantly, you can retain

Your firm has invested in your recruitment and training. They want you to stay. Help them!

your network. If you don't leave elegantly then you can expect to lose any good will and brand equity that you've created. Consider: you are signing up for your *last day*, not the *last word*. If you are going, then go. Just go gracefully.

If you are new to the world of work world, especially to the corporate world, please know that I wrote this book with you in mind. If your job is not going well, please don't be discouraged, please don't be silent about your unhappiness, and please don't quit. Your firm has invested a lot in recruiting and training you. They are interested in keeping you on the team. Please ask yourself if you are doing what I have recommended in this book. Are you working hard on building that network? Are you getting out of your office, or are you hiding in there? Are you joining clubs or otherwise participating in events that help you feel like part of a community? Does anyone know that you are feeling dissatisfied or under-appreciated, or perhaps that you don't feel that you are a member of the team? Please talk to your manager and your mentors. Help them understand where you are, and how to help you. You can do that, without appearing to be whining, by:

If you are leaving, go gracefully. You are signing up for the last day, not the last word.

- Summarizing where you are on your projects, what you have learned, what you have brought to the team, and what the team results are. Remember: you are going to do this in 'net'.

- Stating what you would like to see happen next; i.e, you'd like to be exposed to more people or more business areas, or you would like more responsibility, etc.

- Having some solutions in mind yourself. Please, don't merely dump your dissatisfaction on the manager or mentor. Remember, your goal isn't simply to be heard. You want solutions, and any

139

ideas you can put on the table will only further that goal.

- Always being positive during these conversations, not accusatory.

- Being reasonable. It may not be reasonable to ask for a raise after three months, for example, unless your organization has a time-based pay plan. It is may not be reasonable to ask to become a manager after one year on the job, or an executive after two. It is probably unlikely that you will be asked to run the European office after your first year, and the entire company after five. You can always validate "reasonableness" by investigating the office, division, company, or industry "norms." You can decide that you are a superstar and are going to blow the "norms" out of the water. That's fine, but even for superstars, there are some parameters.

- Following-up by investigating what your management team has done to help, as well as by letting your accomplishments be known. Don't wait for your manager to get back to you. Please agree on the appropriate timing for a further discussion.

When you are unhappy and want a situation to improve, propose reasonable solutions. Don't just complain.

Remember, your firm wants to keep you. Help the organization help you. This is a time to talk specifically about what you need to help you in your transition. Remember, people generally want to help. Do not suffer in silence.

I get raises, but I don't care about the money. It's not money that motivates me.

I must admit that I've heard of this topic, but I haven't actually ever heard these words fall from anyone's lips. This concept may be an urban myth. If it does describe your sentiments, however, by all means tell someone what does motivate you. With limited resources, managers are always looking for ways other than money to motivate employees. If you genuinely feel this way, every manager I know would like to hear from you.

My manager micro-manages. I don't need him to make the 'big calls' for me, I am perfectly capable of making them myself. How do I get him to stop looking over my shoulder?

If you are executing well—and consistently—this really should not routinely happen. You do need to discuss this with your manager, to assure that you both agree on your level of performance. In the meantime, keep your ego under control, and avoid useless power struggles associated with challenges to your leadership or institutional role. Managers generally are privy to more information than their employees, and may be inclined to 'inspect' employee or team decisions based on their more thorough information. While your situation can be remedied, do realize that there will be times when certain calls will not be yours to make. Sometimes you have to salute (and as long as what you are being asked to do is legal, ethical, and moral, you will be expected to do it), and sometimes you get to command. Nobody commands all the time, and everybody salutes sometimes. Likewise, review the chapter on the art of the argument. Keeping your ego in check will also help you to prepare and present arguments rationally. Finally, note that if you are working on a critical project, which is what you want, you cannot be allowed to fail. You will always be subjected to inspection and suggestions. The best way to keep this level of scrutiny at 'tolerable' levels, is to execute successfully.

> *Understand that if you are working on a critical project—which is ideal—you cannot be allowed to fail. Some level of 'micro-management' is to be expected.*

On the uniqueness of me

Nobody understands how smart I am: I am smarter than the guys "training" me.

Egos can really get in the way at the office. There are many smart people walking around on this planet, and there are still more people who are smarter even than they are. Perhaps you have some skills that your "trainer" does not have, but clearly, he has a few that you don't have, otherwise he would not be training you. While he *is* training you, your job is to learn from him. If you are convinced that you are wasting your time with someone who is clearly beneath your acceptable level of interaction intelligence, learn faster, and move on.

What if I am not as smart as everyone else here?

Fantastic! Since there will absolutely positively be people in your organization who are smarter than you are, the best thing you can do for yourself and your team is to consult with and learn from this "brain trust." You don't have to be the smartest person in the room, but you want to be the one who consistently delivers.

Why don't these guys "get excited" about the problems around here?

I especially love energetic and enthusiastic people. However, a very senior member of my own management chain once told a class of new executives, "Don't let yourself get too high, and don't let yourself get too low, because you can't think well from either place." I used to think he was a bit "unexcitable," but with time I came to understand this very, very good advice, which I pass on to you. Don't read or believe your own positive press. Keep a cool head, stay focused on your commitments, and keep going.

Why can't I just be myself here?

I think you can be yourself—to a point. You can't ignore the office culture while you are being yourself, however. Your sense of urgency, your dress, your language, and your work ethic must be in alignment with the leaders of your organization. If your office is fast-paced, with fast walkers, talkers and thinkers, you will not be very successful there if you are of a more leisurely persuasion. Dress for where you happen to be and where you want to go. Accept that while the dress at your branch office is casual, the offices in Dallas or New York may not be; if you have to go to either of these places, you need to dress appropriately for their offices. No matter how casual the office is, it's not the beach or the mall. Please, no excess skin: cover up. There is an office 'lingo', so you should familiarize yourself with it and use it. Finally, with regard to language in general, if it is off-color, it's off-limits.

> *Your sense of urgency, dress, language, and work ethic must be in alignment with the organization's leadership team.*

There is limited growth in the company. Everyone is competing for the same jobs. How can I stand out?

You really don't have to wait for someone to retire to get promoted, even in a slow-growth organization. You do have to distinguish yourself from everyone else, however, if you want to get noticed. A sure-fire way to do this is to have differentiating experiences. For example, if you are an accountant in an accounting department, you can stand out from the others by taking an assignment in the operations department of a business line. You may still be doing accounting work, but now you are looking at one specific business, and you are involved in the day-to-day operations of that business. This will distinguish you from the accountants who spend their careers in the accounting department.

Other ways to distinguish yourself:

- Leave your division or department, then return. Even if you do the same kind of job, you'll have had a unique experience outside your organization, and the organization in turn will benefit from any new skills you'll have acquired.

- Take an assistant's position. (In the corporate world, these are technical assistants or executive assistants.) They usually report to senior management members. Assistants can broadly observe how businesses are run and better prepare to eventually manage one themselves.

- Take a special assignment for six to nine months. If you have executed well in your current assignment, your management team may be open to allowing you to go learn new skills.

- Go back to school to get an advanced degree or complete a certification program. I often hear employees talk about taking classes. Don't just take classes: start a program and finish. If you take classes, you'll be someone who has "taken a few classes." By finishing, you have substantially added to your qualifications.

- Volunteer for task forces, even if doing so doesn't allow you to leave your current position. Make sure that you get some kind of leadership experience out of the task force, and that managers and other leaders who are important to you know about the experience.

- Volunteer to **lead** charitable causes that are important to the organization. If they don't exist, create them. 'Lead' and 'create' are the operative words here. You are not looking for opportunities in which to 'participate,' you

> *Set an educational goal and finish. Don't be someone who 'takes classes'.*

are looking for opportunities to demonstrate leadership.

Everybody wants us to do more with less . . . How can we keep doing this?

Remember the attitude chapter? I put that chapter in for a reason. Some things we can change, some things we cannot. If you can't fix a problem, don't spend a lot of time complaining about it, and do resist listening to those who do. Just keep going, and ask for help when you think your progress is waning. The management team understands funding and resource allocation challenges. They will help where they can. When asking for help, make sure you are specific about what you ask for, and make sure you have some ideas for managing your situation as well. You cannot be "helpless" in the face of your funding or resource crisis. You cannot ask for general help or ask management to solve your problems. You'll get "help" if you don't do well, but it will more than likely be the kind of "help" (intense scrutiny and criticism) most of us would like to avoid.

If you are 'helpless' in a crisis, you get plenty of 'help', but not the kind you will enjoy.

CHAPTER 10

Pulse and Surge:

How to make your vision of you happen

Wherever you work, chances are there is a company program under which you can identify your career aspirations and then devise a plan to achieve them. Under these programs, an employee and manager will meet to discuss the employee's ultimate ambition, identify some tactical actions that the employee needs to take to address some perceived weaknesses, and perhaps devise a timeline under which the employee can—with continued strong execution—potentially achieve his goals. If after these sessions the plan, let's call it a 'Career Development Plan', is filed away and forgotten about until it's time to do another the following year, then nothing positive will happen. In fact, probably nothing at all will happen, because essentially you don't have a plan.

Among the people I have mentored over the years, I've seen many such "paper" development plans. Let's say you want to become Chief Scientist. And let's assume that in general it takes a fair amount of experience to become Chief Scientist, and on average none of the prior Chief Scientists have become Chief Scientists without having had, say, fifteen years of varied research, development, and manufacturing experience. If you write in your Development Plan solely that you want to become Chief Scientist and set a date of fifteen years (minus any relevant experience you may have already had) from the date you write

149

the plan, nothing timely is going to happen. No one, including you, is going to feel any great need to rush to develop you, if your plan gives you a total of fifteen years to declare success. What needs to happen—what you need to *make* happen—is that in addition to declaring that you want to become Chief Scientist, you and your manager or mentors identify a series of positions or experiences you need to have, with specific date ranges for each, culminating in your being prepared and competitive for an appointment to Chief Scientist.

With this plan in place, **you** have to manage your manager on a regular basis to assure that you are both taking the plan seriously, and working according to the plan. With these goals in mind—and on paper—you now need to execute. You also need to excel in your current position, and keep your eye—and your manager's eye—on the next steps you have defined. It's interesting to note that while nothing in your 'Development Plan' is a guarantee, without a detailed plan, you will have a guarantee: that is, that you are less likely to see many timely 'developmental' opportunities.

Don't just fill out forms. Make sure your leadership team is aware of your aspirations and together, devise a plan to make them happen.

Dream big

I have found among my mentees that many of them struggle with defining what it is they ultimately want to do in their careers. I have not yet determined if it is because they are afraid to tell me, or if it's because they don't feel secure enough to dream about what they can potentially achieve. I have an exercise that I propose for these less-than-forthcoming types, one that almost always starts the flow of ideas.

> *If you were giving the keynote for a big industry event, what would you want said about you in your introduction?*

Pretend that you are about to deliver a keynote for a large and important industry event. Thousands of people are in the audience. (At the first sign of panic, I tell them not to focus on their speech or those thousands of people for the moment). I ask them to pretend that I am the host of the event, and I am about to introduce them. What is it that they would like said about themselves? I remind them to keep reality at bay and simply focus on what they would like to hear. I usually relate what I would like to have said about me under the same circumstances.

I like to tell them that when I came up with this exercise about eight years ago, I kicked myself into high gear and finished the master's degree I had started over a decade before, only I went to a more prestigious engineering school. To further encourage them, I tell them how I put myself on the path to becoming an executive at my firm, and began to think about this book.

I've seen many relatively vague or high-level Development Plans get fleshed out with meaningful assignments and aggressive timelines following this exercise. If you think of it as a path to fulfilling your dreams, rather than completing a form, you will free yourself to reach higher, and can place yourself on path to achieve those dreams. Remember, people will help you! A well-written Development Plan is your means of telling them how to help you achieve your goals.

Pulsing and surging

To the extent that you are thinking—seriously thinking—about what you want and what steps *you* can take to make that happen, you are pulsing. While no one can see any action occurring, pulsing by definition means *stuff is happening*. You can pulse over your career or your home life, or whatever it is that you would like to accomplish but have not. Pulsing requires admitting to yourself what it is you really want, and brainstorming on how you can accomplish that. Pulsing requires you to think and identify the steps *you* can take—independently of what others have done before, or what protocol dictates or limits—and create opportunities and a timeline that works for you. Pulsing puts you in the driver's seat, and if you need help, your task is to find it. I like the idea of pulsing specifically for that reason—I get to drive. Surging is a result of all of that pulsing; it's the execution phase. You see real movement and results based on your dreams, brainstorming, and action!

If you're doing the things this book recommends—executing, inspecting, netting, presenting data and yourself effectively, leading, owning, networking, being visible, respectful, and action-oriented, then it's very likely that you are on a path to achieve your career and/or life goals.

If you can and are doing all of these things, real mentors tell you, please get out there a be a real mentor to someone else!

SAMPLE DOCUMENTS

You don't need a lot of words to formulate or report on your business commitments. In fact, your reviewer may not *appreciate* a lot of words, particularly if she has a number of these to read. In any case, you are not being evaluated on how much you write, but rather on whether or not you've achieved the results you committed to deliver.

In developing these documents, please integrate all of the themes we've addressed so far: be net, use leadership language, be factual, specific, and quantitative.

In the following pages, I've included some sample Business Commitment documents, as well as contrasting email samples and a sample Career Development Plan for review.

2007 Annual Business Plan

Business Commitments

Increase client satisfaction rating by ten percentage points by executing on the top three key engagement metrics as defined by the client.

Deliver $10M of revenue and $2.5M of gross profit by 12/15/07. Commit to a stretch revenue plan of $12M and $3M of gross profit.

Grow business segment market share by one percentage point by 4Q by collaborating with the development lab and marketing to announce and release Project Phenomenal by May 15, 2007.

Improve thruput in manufacturing by ten percentage points this fiscal year by introducing the OWNIT (Only When we Need It ,Truly) flow.

Mentoring and Climate

Aggressively mentor new and 'stalled' employees to retain skilled employees while strengthening the organization's leadership bench.

Develop strategies and introduce programs to improve climate and employee morale.

Personal Goals

Complete a word processing course to improve speed and quality of any manuscripts produced.

Figure 5: Sample Business Commitments

2007 Annual Business Plan Results

Business Commitments

Increased client satisfaction rating by seven percentage points by executing on the top two key engagement metrics as defined by the client.

Over-achieved committed revenue and gross profit, delivering $11.5M of revenue and $2.75M of gross profit. These results fall short of the stretch target but exceed the budget revenue and gross profit targets by 15% and 10% respectively.

Due to release delays from the development lab, the marketing team was unable to announce and release Project Phenomenal on May 15, 2007. The announcement and market share attack plan are now slated for 2H2008.

Our extended implementation team successfully released the OWNIT flow in 3Q, resulting in a 12% increase in manufacturing thruput in 4Q. The improvement in thruput enabled the shipment of $5M of incremental revenue this year.

Mentoring and Climate

Developed and introduced 'Mentoring Mojo' for newly hired employees and employees who are not having the success they envisioned for themselves. Hundreds of employees have signed on to 'the mojo' and report feeling more in control of their destinies, and more networked.

Personal Goals

I did not complete a word processing course to improve speed and quality of any manuscripts produced. As a result, I've lost time to market.

Figure 6: Sample Business Results

Career Development Plan

Name:	Excellent Employee
Current Position:	Program Director, Team Tremendous
Within Next Five Years:	VP, Extreme Enterprise
Personal Strengths:	Analytical, energetic, committed, tri-lingual, strong communication skills. Excellent Coach.
Business Strengths:	Project Management, business development, Sales, mentoring
Needs to Demonstrate:	Building organizational capability Thinking Horizontally competency

Next Steps:

Position	Skill Gained	Time-line	Owner
Director, Big Business Product Line	Profit & Loss Building organizational capability	3Q07	Excellent Employee and Marvelous Manager
Director, Entirely New Business Product Line	Building organizational capability Horizontal thinking competency	4Q09	Excellent Employee and Marvelous Manager, Watchful GM
VP, Extreme Enterprise	All of the above, new division	2Q12	Current Watchful GM New Division's GM

Other Skills:

List of skills to be augmented and means to do so:

Complete mini-MBA course: 2Q07

Figure 7: Sample Career Development Plan

Emails: A "Do"

Subject: Project Awesome Resource Allocations/Time

Bob,

In this morning's Operations meeting you asked about Project Awesome's resource growth over time. We are authorized to grow to 20 people by 2008. We have begun hiring and expect to be at eight people on board by year-end.

Please call if you have questions.

Mary

Figure 8: Sample "Do" Email

Emails: A "Don't"

Subject: Your question on Project Awesome today

Bob,

In this morning's Operations meeting you asked about Project Awesome's resource growth over time. We are authorized to grow to 20 people by 2008. This level of growth assumes that we don't experience any funding loss at any time during the project, and you know how unlikely that is, especially in this environment. Please note that we have already been told that our original headcount request of 30 people was unreasonable and that we'd never get that level of resource allocation. I don't think the accountants fully understand how important this project is. That being said, we are going to try to do what we've been asked to do with what amounts to a 33% reduction of resources, before we even start. I've started hiring already and expect to be at eight people on board by year-end, that is, if someone else's project doesn't get re-prioritized over this one. I really need all the engineers I can get. I just hope we can get it all done.

It'll be a miracle!

Please call if you have questions.

Mary

Figure 9: Sample "Don't" Email

AFTERWORD

The Best Of

While I continue to learn a lot from my associates, below are some of the best things I've learned to date from a:

Corporate Lawyer (H. Huberfeld)

Always thank the party you are negotiating with for any concession they make.

Corporate Accountant (All of them)

All the numbers have to add up **and be consistent** page by page and column by column. Rounding is not a good excuse for lack of consistency.

Project Executive (K. Kenlan)

Consistency is better than precision.

Engineering Executive (T. Caulfield)

Answer 'what do you expect to happen?' before you start down an experimental path.

Sales Executive (H. Lasky)

Be an invaluable resource to your client.

Retired executive mentor (H. Geipel)

Inspect Don't Expect!

Karate Instructor (D. Quinlan Sensei)

The mind is weak, but the body is strong. Internalizing this means you can keep going when you are tired and want to give up. You can ignore or coach yourself through self-doubt.

Brazilian Jujitsu Instructor (J. Fernandez)

The best never rest. This means 'don't rest on your laurels'. The competition will continue to work hard and if you want to stay on top, you have to keep working and improving, too.

An older sister (Sandra)

"You said you'd be ready at 8:00, and it's now 8:01, so me and my car are leaving, with you or without you." From this I learned to keep my commitments and be on time. While neither of us knew at the time, all of that early haranguing was really my first enduring lesson in leadership!

Thank you, Sandy.

Contact the author.

Thank you for purchasing this book.

If you'd like to provide feedback to the author, or have Regina Darmoni address your organization, please contact her via email at **darmoni @realmentorstellyouthis.com.**